Doing Theology with Humility, Generosity, and Wonder

Doing Theology with Humility, Generosity, and Wonder

A Christian Theology of Pluralism

Damayanthi Niles

FORTRESS PRESS

MINNEAPOLIS

DOING THEOLOGY WITH HUMILITY, GENEROSITY,
AND WONDER
A Christian Theology of Pluralism

Cover artwork: Radhika Niles

Cover design: Emily Drake

Paperback ISBN: 978-1-5064-3359-2

eBook ISBN: 978-1-5064-3360-8

To my siblings,
Radhika N.
and Dharman P.
Niles
Who have walked life's journeys with me

And to
my guru, Wendy Doniger
and
my Doktorvater, David Tracy
Whose intellectual DNA have shaped me more than I
even realized.

ACKNOWLEDGMENTS

This book has been gestating in me for many years and many people have been involved in bringing it to fruition.

The amazing community of Asian scholars that filled my home ever since I can remember, generations of family friends that were committed to the work of understanding and articulating theology in a complex and rich world, many of whom are the warp and weft out of which this book is created.

My family, generations of remarkable people who thought deeply about their faith. My parents D. Preman and Sherina P. Niles, my first and truest teachers for nurturing in me curiosity about the world and the love of the One who brought it into being. My siblings Radhika Naomi and Dharmaputhiran Premanandan, to whom this book is dedicated, who have supported me in this and many other journeys.

Eden Seminary colleagues, who have been generous in the valuing of my work and providing the space and place to do it. A particular thanks to Deb Krause, Christopher Grundy, and Kristen Leslie, who have been all that one could ask for as colleagues. Eden students, who have let me try out my ideas on them, asked important questions, and pushed me to look in new directions. The Eden Board, not only for the provision of a generous sabbatical plan that gives space and support for scholarship, but their demand for teaching excellence that always improves scholarship.

My community of friends, in particular Tina Newberry, Diane O'Brien, and Cari Frus, who have prayed for me, cajoled, and cheered me through this process over the years. Dale Bishop and Paul Knitter, who have listened to different versions of the outline of this book as we participated in the Limper program together. Rebecca Ragland and Ben Menghini, who read drafts and gave feedback that greatly helped with clarity.

Finally, a heartfelt thank you to my research assistant extraordinaire, Brett Palmer. He was everything that the nomenclature implies and more. He chased down every obscure idea that came to mind, helped me sift through those ideas, demanded clarity, and provided the metronome that kept me accountable through the long months of writing. The realization of this book is as much a result of his hard work as mine. I truly believe it would have not come together without him.

CONTENTS

PREFACE

There was an incident from my childhood that has shaped the course of my study and work. I was in about seventh grade. I remember standing at the wall at the boarding school that I attended in South India alongside a friend of mine. We were watching the parade of the local goddess through the streets. It was a moving display of devotion and faithfulness of the worshippers to the divine in their midst. My friend commented, "Isn't it lovely? It is too bad they are all damned." I was shocked. I could not understand how the God whom I had been raised to worship should condemn all of these faithful people. It sent me down a path to learn how people of the Christian faith relate to people of other faiths. This book is very much the fruit of that pursuit.

This book looks at how Christians can think about their own theology in a manner that will not only allow them to be more open to interfaith dialogue, but also see that conversation as essential to who we are. Christian theology has, for much of history, been used to undergird and justify imperial power. This desire has required a theological construction that puts forward a vision of belief that stands above and against the world and other faiths, or at the very least acts as the one vision under which all the others must unite. Empire and the colonizing enterprise do not lend themselves well to plural ways of understanding the faith, let alone a plurality of faiths. To take plurality seriously, we need a Christian theology that sees itself as a participant in that plurality.

To do this, I have turned largely to the Asian theologians. Asian Christians, with the notable exception of the Filipinos, are a religious minority in their countries. This reality has made it difficult for them to see themselves apart from people of other faiths, nor do they any longer have the colonial might to assert themselves over or dismiss their religious neighbors. They have to relate to them.

The Sri Lankan theologian Aloysius Pieris, in his book *An Asian Theology of Liberation,* says that for Asian theologians to do their work in a manner that is authentic to their context, they must take two issues seriously. The first is the plurality that makes up Asia. The second is the oppressive poverty that cripples Asia and what it means to be liberated from it.

It is my contention that when we take plurality seriously, we are able to address poverty and bring a word of liberation to the context. The problem with a single arching narrative that attempts to override plurality is that it silences the competing narratives around it. The narratives that are silenced are often those that belong to the weakest who do not have the power to assert their narratives over and against the narrative of the powerful.

In the upcoming chapters, I will look at what it means to think about key theological doctrines in a manner that takes pluralism and liberation seriously. The first chapter looks at God and attributes of God that allow us to be open to pluralism. The second chapter looks at Jesus Christ and how to address this particular incarnation in a manner that enhances our ability to see multiple contexts and expressions of the incarnation, rather than dismissing or choosing between them. The third chapter looks at how the Holy Spirit enables connections across differences. Chapter four addresses plurality within the human being itself. Finally, chapter five looks both at what it means to be Church as a diverse community in the midst of a plurality of communities and the Church's purpose among those communities. In so doing, it is my intent to show how attention to plurality can be a way to address issues of liberation and resist the colonizing impulse. It is my firm belief that by doing theology with the humility to see the plurality of the divine expression around us and the generosity to learn from it, rooted in a sense of awe at the magnificence of God and God's creation, we become authentic practitioners of our Christian faith.

CHAPTER 1

GOD IN A PLURALISTIC WORLD

When we begin any discussion about God, a good starting point is thinking about the language we use to describe God. Why do we name God or anything for that matter? Naming is more than a description. It is a way we claim a relationship with what we describe. When parents name their child, they not only describe the child but make a connection with it. Nicknames function in a similar manner. The giving and accepting of nicknames says a great deal about the relationship or the lack thereof.

Naming, particularly when naming God, helps us find our place in the plurality of relationships that are possible. It speaks to how we see God from the vantage point of *our* relationship. It allows us to be concrete about what we know about God from our particular relationship with the divine without having to presume or require universal knowledge or presume that all the relationships God has are of the same character as the one we have. For example, when we call God a sovereign, it says a great deal about the role God plays in our lives. We connect to God and God connects to us as a ruler to whom we have allegiance. We believe that

God has the ability to tell us what to do for our well-being and that of everyone, and we in turn allow ourselves to be ruled for that purpose. This does not, however, mean that God cannot relate to us in other ways or can only connect to others in a sovereign-subject relationship.

The very nature of language is that it is concrete. Language is necessary for description and to mediate relationships, but no particular language can do it all. We need language to describe reality, but a single language cannot exhaust all that can be said about reality, particularly a reality such as God that transcends all languages, let alone a particular one. Every kind of language reveals different kinds and means of relationship and understanding, and the language we use is a concrete contribution to the plurality of possibilities of relating to and knowing God. Stephen Bevans, in his book *Models of Contextual Theology*, gives the example of the word *rice*. English has only one word for rice, whereas Filipino has different words not only for the grain as it is about to be harvested, drying in the sun, or cooked on the table but also for different preparations and types of rice.[1] Filipino allows an expansion of the concept of rice that is not provided for in English. When Japanese theologian Masao Takenaka claims that God *is* rice in his book with this same title,[2] there is a depth of wisdom to this idea available to a speaker of Filipino that is not as self-evident in solely English expression.

---

[1] Stephen B. Bevans, *Models of Contextual Theology* (Maryknoll, New York: Orbis Books, 2002), 4

[2] MasaoTakenaka, *God is Rice: Asian Culture and Christian Faith* (Geneva: World Council of Churches), 1986.

Raimon Pannikar, in his book *The Experience of God,* argues that discourse about God is unique to all other discourse because it is the naming of reality itself. Because reality itself is beyond the limitations of language, silence is the best means to address God. Unfortunately, silence is not a medium in which one can communicate; therefore, we are dependent on language.[3] When we use language for God, what we are trying to name is the essence of God as it radiates to us through God's relationship to the cosmos. This is a cataphatic approach[4] to giving language to God that compliments Panikkar's apophatic approach that leads to silence.

The function of naming God is to make God intelligible to the finite and is therefore critical both in the experience and understanding of God. Naming God in a way that is authentic to the infinite reality of God is to realize that what we say is but a piece of the infinite reality to which we speak. We need to speak about our piece of the infinite in order to share our experience and at the same time do so in a manner that allows us to be open to other possibilities that have not occurred to us. For example, when we say God is beauty, the finite concept of beauty is pressed

---

[3]   Raimon Panikkar, *The Experience of God: Icons of the Mystery* (Minneapolis: Fortress Press, 2006), 12–13.

[4]   The cataphatic approach to God talk is the discipline of understanding God by naming what God reveals about Godself. The assumption is that what radiates out of God provides the best basis for names for God. Apophatic language starts with the assumption that all language is limited when it comes to talking about the divine. It looks at the limits of names of God by showing God simultaneously claims, negates, and overwhelms the terms that are used for God.

beyond its limited definition as aesthetically pleasing or perfect to the senses to an infinite sense that pushes the idea to the edges of its conceptual reality until the finite sense of the term completely fails to define it. As our sense of beauty is stretched, so our sense of God is stretched. So, God is beauty and more than beauty. Beauty becomes more of what we understood the word to ever mean because of its association with God. When listening to music, we often understand beauty as a major chord. We can stretch to hear the dis-ease of a minor chord as beautiful, but can a dissonant chord be beautiful? Where is the hidden, unheard beauty of such a chord? Just as our idea of beautiful chords are stretched from simple major chords to include unpleasurable harmonies, so our names for God are stretched by infinite reality to unconsidered ways of understanding the terms we use for naming God. In other words, it is simultaneously true that God is beauty, God is not beauty, and God is not not beauty.[5] This apophatic stretching of language pushes it beyond its finite bounds and leads us, as Panikkar notes, into a richer and deeper silence into which language disappears.

That is why the means by which we talk about God is through symbols. As Panikkar notes, the names we use for God are symbols.[6] They are words that point to and give limited insight into what they describe. This is in opposition, Panikkar says, to concepts that presume to describe the reality itself as it actually is. Symbols point beyond

---

[5]   For more on this approach to apophaticism see: The Liturgists, "God Our Mother," *The Liturgists Podcast*, Podcast audio, May 6, 2014, http://www.theliturgists.com/god-our-mother/.

[6]   Panikkar, *Experience of God*, 17.

themselves, concepts point to themselves.[7] In his article, *Together and Uniqueness—Living Faith in Inter-Relation*, Sri Lankan theologian Lakshman Wickremesinghe notices that different faith groups are taking a new attitude toward their own founders and scriptures. They have become aware that while their insights are uniquely central and normative for all, they are not necessarily complete and total in their wisdom.[8] It is precisely this kind of assumption that underlies the focus on symbolic language when referencing God. Symbols allow us to say something about God that is central and normative without the assumption that it is complete and total in its understanding. They are the best means of attending to the infinite because they reveal and veil it in the same moment. They allude to a reality rather than explain it, which is critical when talking about something that defies description or explanation. As Panikkar goes on to state, symbols uproot absolutism and make "impossible every totalitarianism of whatever type there may be."[9] Whatever we say we know, there is more than we can imagine to be said. For these reasons, we can never speak as if we have put forward the complete and final understanding. This is extremely helpful for finite beings wanting to talk about things they can never understand in their infinite totality.

Symbols also imply relationship. They require a connection between the one who uses the symbol and the one

---

[7]   Panikkar, *Experience of God*, 17.

[8]   Lakshman Wickremesinghe, "Togetherness and Uniqueness-Living Faiths in Inter-Relation," *CTC Bulletin* 5, no. 1–2 (April-August, 1984): 7.

[9]   Panikkar, *Experience of God*, 15.

whom the symbol refers to. Symbols say as much about the one making the reference as the reference itself. They also say something about the connection between them. The symbol has meaning in the immediate moment. At the same time, as the relationship between the one using the symbol and the one whom it refers to evolves, the very nature of the symbol evolves. An example of this is the often used symbol of God as Father. There is something very concrete and specific about this symbol that says as much, if not more, about the one using it to refer to God as it does about God who is being referred to. Furthermore, a toddler's relationship to its father is different from that of the same child at the age of nine, fourteen, thirty, or fifty. The relationship with the parent evolves and so the meaning of the symbol, father, also changes over time. Finally, because it is being used in reference to God, it invites the one using the symbol of "father" to press deeper into what that relationship can and does mean and how God is more than that definition of relationship.

Paul Ricœur outlines two guidelines to discern symbols in his book, *Symbolism of Evil.*[10] First, symbols give rise to thought that gives space to ruminate about a concept without actually explaining it. That allows us, the users of the symbol, and God, the one which the symbol points to, the space to have the dynamic relationship by which the symbol is continuously shaped, as in the example above. Second, related symbols and previous uses of the same symbol affect the meaning of each other. There is often a dominant meaning to a symbol. However, a symbol holds the essence of the manner in which it was used in the past,

---

[10]   Paul Ricouer, *Symbolism of Evil* (Boston: Beacon Press, 1967), 351.

which continues to give a patina to the way it is used now. It is rather like a container that holds essential oil. Even if the container is washed and a new oil is put in, some shadow of the previous oil remains. Symbols are also affected by the meanings of similar symbols used in a different context. So the Greek construction of Zeus as father affects the use of father to understand God in our tradition. The same is true of the use of the language of fatherhood in other traditions, particularly in reference to the divine. Also, different languages of masculinity in different contexts affect the symbol of fatherhood that in turn affects the symbol of God as father. Symbols of parenting add more layers and so forth. In other words, the etymology of a symbol is going to affect the symbol as much as its immediate meaning, the subject that is using it, the object for which it is being used, and the relationship between them. This is the thick means of discourse indeed.

The question before us is: what symbols for God help us to address the plurality in which we find ourselves? The Sri Lankan scholar Aloysius Pieris notes that the context that has plurality at the center of its awareness is Asia. Asia is a context in which, by and large, the Christian faith is a minority tradition. Not only do many religious traditions and ideologies coexist next to each other, but it is a continent of many ethnic groups, languages, cultures, geographies, and world views. It could be said that the one thing Asians have in common is nothing. The other reality of Asia, notes Pieris, is a context that needs to attend to crippling poverty. He believes an authentic Christian theology in Asia must deal with the dual issues of pluralism and liberation. In his words, we must be "baptised in the Jordan of Asian religion [plurality] and on the cross of Asian poverty [liberation]."[11] It is the contention of this author that it is only through the embracing of plurality that true liberation can be found. The streamlining of plurality is often at the cost of the voices who do not have the power to assert themselves in the dominant vision. They are therefore silenced and dismissed.

In this book, we are asking questions about what names for God allow us to relate to God in ways that not only see the plurality around us but also how God attends to that plurality by working to liberate and celebrate it rather than suppressing and controlling it. This requires a contextual approach to theology. Contextual theology, by definition, starts by reading the context and then making deductions. The simple fact is that creation is fundamentally plural. There are many kinds of everything in creation. I am reminded of a conversation I had with the Japanese theologian Kosuke Koyama. He had returned from taking his grandson to a petting zoo that boasted having every species of chicken in the world. He was laughing and saying, "So many chickens? Why do we need so many chickens? What a wasteful abundance!" What a wasteful abundance indeed. There are many kinds of chickens, birds, trees, flowers and, yes, human beings. Scientists tell us that if there are not many kinds of a species, then that species is easily wiped out. This was the fate of the Dutch Elm tree due to the Dutch elm disease until a resistant strain of the tree could be found. Plurality simply is.

---

11   Aloysius Pieris, *An Asian Theology of Liberation* (Edinburgh: T & T Clark, 1988), 50.

The question that needs to be asked is: what is God's relationship to plurality? I see three possible responses to this question. The first is that plurality is not God's intention but God's mistake, implying the need for correction. In other words, God created the world plural but wants it to be unified under a single reality and works to make it so. In this view, it's almost as if God tried different things at first and now has to organize all of the variations into one single correct vision. A lot of our language about creation that speaks of ordering and taming chaos leans in this direction. It assumes that chaos is bad and creation is the good that is made by controlling or eliminating the chaos.

A second response is that plurality is a result of human brokenness, also implying the need for correction. One example of this is the common exegesis of the Tower of Babel text. The dominant tradition of interpretation views humanity's movement inward as sinful hubris in the face of God. God's response is thus interpreted as punishing or even cursing humanity with plurality. Underpinning this interpretation is the assumption that the ideal state of humanity is the prior state of humanity: with "one language and the same words," and the divine punishment was the destruction of that state.[12]

The third response is that plurality is a part of God's intention and creation is purposely fashioned in that manner. Wesley Ariarajah gives biblical rationale for leaning toward

---

[12] I will return to this interpretation of the Tower of Babel and explore alternative interpretations in chapter 3.

the intentional plurality of creation.[13] God creates the universe and provides for it. Genesis talks about all of humankind and not just a specific race or people. The Psalms, particularly Psalm 104, speak of God's providential care for all of creation. The Psalmist sees creation as an ongoing activity of God, not just an activity of the past. Since the creative work that God continues to do expands plurality rather than correcting it toward uniformity, the plurality of creation is not a mistake but was intended by God from the beginning. Ariarajah goes on to say that the Barthian overemphasis on incarnation leaves an impoverished doctrine of creation. Creation in Karl Barth's theology seems to become the faulty material that is to be corrected and ordered by the incarnation. It follows the theme in Oscar Cullmann's salvation history that describes God's salvific activity in the Bible and ordering of history as a narrowing from universal creation to the particular person of Jesus Christ and then expanding out again. In this version of salvation history, God's story begins with creation and then begins to narrow. It narrows with Noah, losing all other living beings. It narrows further with Abraham, losing Lot and his descendants. It narrows again with Isaac, losing Ishmael, the father of Islam. It narrows with the loss of the northern kingdom to the Assyrians (from whence the Samaritans arise), with those taken into exile, losing those who were left in Jerusalem, and then with those who return from exile, losing those left behind in Babylon. The story narrows finally to the redemptive one, Christ. Cullmann

---

13   S. Wesley Ariarajah, *Your God, My God, Our God: Rethinking Christian Theology for Religious Plurality* (Geneva: World Council of Churches Publications, 2012), 49–51.

then argues that salvation broadens out again through those who believe in the sacrificial death and resurrection of Jesus Christ, to the whole world through the missional work of the Church, and in particular the Church that is based in Rome, western Europe and the United States. The movement of salvation history is from the many to the one and then back to the many—with the pivotal role played by Christ. Christ then becomes the one who makes meaning of all that went before and after.[14] Creation as the source of general revelation is understood by Barthians as a hopeless means to understand God since humans' sinfulness makes it impossible for them to see God in creation. Jesus Christ alone can tell us who God is and make sense of the world. Jesus Christ is not only a central and normative means of making meaning but the complete and total one.

The Psalms' description of creation, by contrast, are notable for their inclusion of the whole cosmos. They are not sectarian in addressing where God's creative and provisional work manifests itself, rather they celebrate its presence among all people and all creation. Even the election, promise, and revelation that is centered on the Jewish people in the Torah does not override God's relationship to the whole world.[15] If plurality is intentional, it shapes the way we construct our theology. It brings God's whole creation to the center of the construction. Our theological constructions need to be shaped by the plurality around us and help us find our particular place in conversation with that plurality.

---

[14] Oscar Cullmann, *Christ and Time*, trans. Floyd V. Filson (Philadelphia: Westminster Press, 1949), 93.

[15] Ariarajah, *Your God*, 49–51.

So, what is helpful language to describe God that takes that plurality seriously? If we start with the creation, which has already been posited as plural, how does that help us to understand and name God? Lakshman Wickremesinghe suggests that there are five dominant symbols that convey basic biblical insights regarding God's relation to creation.[16] The first symbol is the divine as an initiating creative energy motivated by love and care for that which it creates. The second is that there is a purpose and vision for creation aiming for what is good, meaningful, and beautiful. The third symbol is finitude. The creator's infinite nature is shared in a finite way in creation. The fourth is contingency. All of creation is dependent on God for its existence. The fifth symbol is that God finds a way to guide the creative process to completion, particularly in the cross-bearing rec-reation process.

The key insight to help us with our work is the third one, that of the relation of the finite to the infinite. Creation is a finite expression of God's infinite nature. If creation is plural, then God is infinitely so. God's nature is infinitely plural. This way of thinking gives us space to think of mystery as infinite possibilities of plurality. This also gives us space to re-evaluate our understanding of chaos. Chaos becomes a way to name the infinity of possibilities for plurality that are in God. An infiniteness of possibility for plurality is chaotic. By its very nature it overwhelms the finite possibilities, throwing finitude into the mystery out of which it is made. It is important to note that this chaotic nature is not something to be feared and corrected but embraced as the

---

16   Lakshman Wickremesinghe, "Christianity Moving Eastwards," *CTC Bulletin* 5, no. 1–2 (April-August, 1984): 65–66.

very essence of the Mystery that created us and into which we are returned. Is it a wonder that Panikkar says silence is the best language for God? But in the need of words to communicate, Mystery and Chaos are useful names to use to understand God, particularly in relation to plurality.[17]

Another helpful name when thinking about God in connection to plurality is relational. God is a relational being and how God relates is seen in how God creates and relates to that creation. Wesley Ariarajah explores biblical language about God in creation.[18] Creation is the place that God's handiwork is seen and reflexively how God's wisdom, compassion, and greatness are discerned. He lifts up three images of how God creates the cosmos in the Bible. First, the cosmos is formed and fashioned by God. Creation is not an accident but has deliberate intention and fore-thought. God wanted to make creation the way God made it. It gives creation a preciousness and value to God. To use the language of liberation, no part of it is of lesser value, needing to be suppressed or exploited for another or even the whole. The second image Ariarajah puts forward is that creation radiates from God. What we see in a finite manner in creation, we presume, is in an infinite manner in God. That is why we can say if creation is created plural, it carries the imprint of a God who is an infinite version of creation, hence infinitely plural. It reflects something about God in the way it is fashioned. Third, it is for the enjoyment and play of God, rather than the need of God. There is a tone of want, desire, and delight rather than need, requirement, and

---

[17] I will explore chaos in relationship to God further, specifically in relationship to the Holy Spirit, in chapter 3.

[18] Ariarajah, *Your God*, 53–55.

duty in this idea that speaks to God's enjoyment of creation. Hinduism has a lovely concept of creation as Leela, which means the laughter and play of God. This idea is reflected in this biblical theme. Ariarajah points out that none of these biblical themes are sectarian. None of them give preference to one part, people or race over the rest. All of it is created by God and connected to God.

The ideas go even deeper when one considers *what* God formed and fashioned creation out of. Christian thought posits two possibilities, God creates out of nothing (*ex-nihilo*) or preexisting matter. Both these options make the substance out of which creation is formed something other than God. Lakshman Wickremesinghe draws on Hindu philosophy to suggest a deeper connection and relationship between God and creation that echoes the radiation language that Ariarajah points to in the Bible. The symbol Wickremesinghe uses is creation *ab divino*, "within God." The root image is *Sakti*, energy overflowing from the divine abundance that results in creation. The *Sakti-Uma* describes creation as emerging specifically from the womb of God and existing in the plenitude of life. God is actually creating creation from God's self. Wickremesinghe layers two more concepts onto this symbol: *Hiranyagarbha*, the Golden Germ out of which the creation emerges and *Prajapati*, the source of creation giving out of itself for others from the recesses of the Ultimate. The concepts add the language of sacrifice and self-giving to the symbol system.[19] The Golden Germ must break open from its self-containment to bring forth more life.

---

[19]   Wickremesinghe, "Christianity Moving Eastwards," 66–67.

Wickermesinghe argues that this *Sakti-Uma* idea of creating enriches the biblical symbols of creation by deepening the inherently personal and intimate relationships of creation to God. It also provides a sense of an interiorized and pervasive presence of God that echoes the panentheism found in Christian Orthodox traditions.[20] It is a kind of radical immanence that helps enrich the idea of transcendence. Transcendence is about a God who is in all of creation but not contained by it. It fits the apophatic vision so central to the mystics. It also gives clarity to an idea of God as immanent and transcendent in and at the same time. The idea of *Sakti-Uma* also gives a new layer to the idea of separation and sin. Breaking covenant with God is more than just the betrayal of a legal relationship between a king and a subject as emphasized by St. Anselm's theory of atonement or even as emphasized in images of Jesus as the sacrificial lamb.[21] Through the lens of *Sakti-Uma*, cross-sacrifice is seen in light of God's womb-like love, moving us from a legal to a parental metaphor. God is a heartbroken parent, desperate to bring one's child back into healthy relationship.

Another symbol that helps illuminate the connection between relationality, plurality, and even liberation is the Christian concept of God as Trinity. If God is a Trinity, then God in Godself is relational plurality. The different elements of God come together to make God God. They are all of equal importance to the whole. It is the relationship between the plurality in the Godhead that overflows and makes creation. Creation in turn, echoing the relationships out of which it is made, is in itself relational and plural. This

---

20   Wickremesinghe, "Christianity Moving Eastwards," 68.

21   Wickremesinghe, "Christianity Moving Eastwards," 68.

thickens the *Sakti-Uma* idea that God creates out of Godself and therefore creation has God's nature.

We can use Trinitarian language to think about liberation. Whenever we diminish or lose any part of the Godhead, our image of God is diminished and no longer looks like God. Similarly, when any part of the plurality of the creation is diminished or lost, creation itself, like the God who created it, is diminished or lost and no longer looks like creation as it was intended to be. The language of mystery and relationship not only open us to the plurality in God and creation but also the value and purpose of liberation. An infinitely plural God who creates a world in God's image with intention and forethought would champion that plurality. Liberation in this sense would mean empowering the parts of that plural world that are suppressed and admonishing the ones who do the suppressing, with the goal of bringing them into healthy relationships with each other as they are meant to be. That requires honoring plurality and being enriched by it, rather than abrogating it or being divided by it. In this way, creation becomes a finite representation of the God out of which it was made.

CHAPTER 2

CHRIST IN A PLURALISTIC WORLD

The way for Christians to enter into the mystery of and re-lationship with God is through Christology. Christology is all about incarnation, which God made clear in a particular place and time. Steven Bevans states that doing theology contextually is imperative and part of the very nature of theology itself.[1] Theology out of context is vacuous. It does not take seriously the situation the theology is being articulated in and as a result, becomes unintelligible. Bevans tells the story of preparing an Advent liturgy using the metaphor of the sun, which brings light and warmth to the darkness, to describe how Christ brings light and warmth to the world. This evocative image from a temperate climate was lost on his Indian colleague, for whom the sun is not connected to renewal in the same way. For his colleague, the sun was a source of punishing, baking heat from which one needed to escape. It caused thirst and sunstroke.[2] Although, the historical use of Christ as a colonizing tool might indeed

---

[1] Stephen B. Bevans, *Models of Contextual Theology*, rev. ed. (Maryknoll: Orbis Books, 2002), 3.

[2] Bevans, *Models,* xix.

have made this a perfect image for how Christ came to his shores!

Universalized theological language is susceptible to becoming a tool of the powerful. It is imposed on situations by the powerful. The symbol of Christ, the cross, has been used time after time to colonize land, people, resources, and even ideas in the name of the powerful. Douglas Hall in *The Cross in Our Context* tells the story of Jacques Cartier sailing up the St Lawrence River in what is now Canada and planting a cross on the top of a small mountain on the site of a Mohawk village and claiming it for the king of France.[3] For this story, there are thousands more like it. Universal theological language is unhelpful at best and dangerous at its worst.

That being said, the fear of those who cling to universal absolutes is that without such absolutes one falls into relativism. The worry is that if you do not have a single clear idea, you have chaos or nothing. The truth is, as we have seen in the previous chapter, chaos is the source of creative possibility. It is at the heart of mystery. It is also only when you have multiplicity (whether it be creatures, contexts, or ideas) that they can relate to each other. Perhaps that is why we place a multiplicity in the very heart of the Godhead. The question then becomes, how do these multiplicities relate and inform each other? This question will be addressed later in the chapter.

If universalism is a problem for theology in general, it is much more for Christology since this doctrine is about how God becomes finite in a context. Indian theologian

---

3   Douglas John Hall, *The Cross in Our Context* (Minneapolis: Fortress Press, 2003), 36.

Justice P. Chenchiah argues against universalism saying that it, by its very nature, thwarts the historical reality that is at the very heart of the Christological idea.[4] Why is it we abstract and universalize what we have learned about Christ among particular people and turn it into universal ideological principles? We too often look at the work of Christ in terms of what it does for all. In so doing, we fail to see how the context from which any wisdom arises shapes that ideal vision in a particular way.

The value of Christology is that it is about incarnation. God is immanent in particular ways such that we who are finite can have access to the infinite. In Christology, God is made contextual and therefore is best understood in the contexts in which God is manifest.

African theologians use indigenous metaphors to contextualize Christological themes. Anne Nasimiyu-Wasike outlines five basic Christological themes found in the African context.[5] The first theme is the eschatological, which understands Christ as the one who comes to die in an alienated world. In the act of resurrection, he shows he is victor over the forces that alienate the world. The second theme is the anthropological, which sees Christ as called and calling us to a lifestyle that is dedicated to love of neighbor as a means to nurture life. The third theme is the liberator. Here, Christ is the one who works to eliminate suffering and create a better world for all. The fourth theme is that of

---

[4] M. M. Thomas, *The Acknowledged Christ of the Indian Renaissance* (London: SCM Press Ltd, 1969), 161–164.

[5] Anne Nasimiyu-Wasike, "Christology and an African Woman's Experience," in *Faces of Jesus in Africa*, ed. Robert J. Schreiter (Maryknoll: Orbis Books, 1991), 70–81.

cosmological restorer, where Christ is viewed as one who restores everything to God. In the broken world, humanity has moved out of its place and dominates the world. Once the world is reconciled, humanity moves back to its appropriate cosmological place. The fifth model is healer. Here, Christ is understood as the one who restores individuals and communities to health.[6]

These themes become even richer as they become indigenized. Anselme Sanon talks about the idea of Jesus as the eldest brother who goes through the initiation rite on behalf of all his siblings so that he can help guide the others through them.[7] We can look at the themes put forward by Nasimiyu-Wasike through this indigenous vision of Christ. The initiation is a ritualized death that overcomes forces that kept the initiate in old ways so that they can step into something new, a symbol system that grounds Nasimiyu-Wasike's eschatological model. The initiation can also be seen as restoring the correct cosmic order. Sanon's exploration of Jesus as the big brother initiate who goes through the initiation rite and therefore is able to guide others through it fleshes out what it means to see Jesus as the one who calls us to love the neighbor, nurture and heal life, and eliminate suffering.

Another indigenous image of Christ, put forward by François Kabasélé, is the metaphor of Jesus as the fully realized Chief.[8] The chief is the son of the Chief and holds au-

---

[6]   Nasimiyu-Wasike, "Christology," 77–80.

[7]   Anselme T. Sanon, "Jesus Master of Initiation," in *Faces of Jesus in Africa*, ed. Robert J. Schreiter (Maryknoll: Orbis Books, 1991), 93.

[8]   François Kabasélé, "Christ as Chief" in *Faces of Jesus in Africa*, ed. Robert J. Schreiter (Maryknoll: Orbis Books, 1991), 103–115.

thority and governs. The language of chief is also connected with language about heroes. A hero in this vision of chief is one who conquers evil and never flees, a pillar of support for the community and emissary of *the* Chief, God. This is another indigenous way of elucidating the metaphor of the cosmic restorer. The chief also proves his power by being able to provide for his people by feeding them, interpreting what it means to be liberator and healer as well.[9]

To put it simply, these are African metaphors for Christ that give substance and breadth to Christological themes that are not possible to see as well in abstract universal forms. The function of metaphor is very much the same as the function of symbol discussed in the chapter about God. Metaphors imply a relationship to the context in which they are used. They say as much about the one making the reference as the reference itself. When speaking about incarnation, this is of critical importance because it grounds the themes in a place. The previous ways the metaphor was used in multiple contexts inform each other and the metaphor itself. The big brother initiate speaks to the theme of the eschatological Christ and the ways the theme was picked up in other metaphors like the Anselmian atonement metaphor from eleventh-century Europe. It deepens, disturbs, and questions both the theme of the eschatological Christ and the other metaphors used to address that theme. As does the incarnate Christ it describes, the metaphor allows the context to illuminate the theme and the theme to illuminate the context.

The other thing one sees when looking at the African metaphors for describing Christ is the focus on community.

---

9   Kabasélé, "Christ," 104–112.

The work of the Christological figures is for the purpose of the community and making it whole. This communal sensibility is obvious in the theme of Christ the healer but is present in all the other themes also. The eschatological Christ comes to champion an alienated world and break the alienating forces by overcoming the death they induce. The anthropological Christ's function is to reconnect neighbors in love and nurture life. The same can be said of the liberator Christ and the eschatological Christ. The communal nature of Christ's work is a key emphasis of the African context and an important contribution to the discussion of Christology as a whole.

Latin Americans, rather than turning to indigenous metaphors to contextualize Christology, turn to social analysis. Leonardo Boff states that there are two types of social analysis.[10] One from the dominant class has a functionalist vision of society, which reinforces the status quo. It talks about society as a healthy organic whole that naturally moves toward balance and equilibrium. It has confidence in the structural support that keep that equilibrium in place. The second kind of social analysis is from what Boff calls the dominated classes. They see society as deeply flawed, fraught with contradictions and blockages. Boff calls this a dialectic vision that stresses struggle and conflict. If the vision of the dominant class sees movement through society as a labyrinth, the dominated class see it as a maze with impenetrable blocks and traps.

---

[10] Leonardo Boff, *Jesus Christ Liberator: A Critical Christology for Our Time*, trans. Patrick Hughes (Maryknoll: Orbis Books,1978), 273–274.

Christ, Boff believes, works out of the dialectical approach of the dominated in society.[11] Jesus had a conflicted relationship with his society, interrupting it and breaking with the status quo so much so he was killed for it.

Saúl Trinidad[12] takes social analysis even further by arguing that the Christology that the Spaniards brought to Latin America was shaped by a long struggle with the Arab empires that colonized them episodically for eight centuries.[13] He argues that once the struggles between the Spanish Christians and Arabic Muslims were over, Ferdinand and Isabella of Spain believed that the means of peace and freedom from oppression was a unified Spain for Christ and Christians that expanded to bring everything under that vision through conquest.[14] Ironically, the Christology they exported was that of a dominated people now using that same Christology to justify dominating others out of fear of being in the persecuted position again. In other words, the Christology of the colonizer is actually the language of an oppressed people who are now doing the oppressing themselves.[15] The powerful insight of Trinidad is that liberation of the oppressed is not enough. There is a healing that is required that allows the oppressed to see themselves, and be seen, as something other than the oppressed, as the *imago dei*. What that means is the vision of Christology that is needed in the struggle to break down an oppressive system

---

[11]   Boff, *Jesus Christ*, 274-293.

[12]   Saúl Trinidad, "Christology, *Conquista,* Colonization," in *Faces of Jesus: Latin American Chrsitologies*, ed. José Miguel Bonino, trans. Robert R. Barr (Maryknoll: Orbis Books, 1984), 49–65.

[13]   Trinidad, "Christology," 49.

[14]   Trinidad, "Christology," 54.

[15]   Trinidad, "Christology," 54.

has to be both one that participates in the conflict, as well as helps the people in that conflict to heal and see themselves and society differently from the ways imagined by the oppressive system. Otherwise the Christology of the oppressed can, as in the case of the Spanish *conquista*, become a Christology of domination.

African Americans also do a social economic analysis to contextualize Christology, but they add the insight of race in shaping that reality. According to James Cone, the father of Black Theology, "The historical Jesus emphasizes the social context of Christology and thereby establishes the importance of Jesus's racial identity. Jesus was a Jew!"[16] It was who Jesus was as a Jew in Jesus's historical moment that connects to who he is in the present historic moment and where he places himself not only economically but racially.[17] This in turn shapes the understanding of the Christ of the eschaton.[18]

It is interesting to speculate what would happen if Latin American Christologies had the same awareness of race that we see in African-American Christologies. Could this additional racial layer help give rise to indigenous metaphors of expressing Christology out of the Latin American context and provide even greater contextual nuances for understanding Christ? This perhaps could give rise to, for example, Mayan or Incan Christologies as opposed to solely Roman Catholic or Protestant visions.

---

[16] James H. Cone, *God of the Oppressed* (San Francisco: Harper, 1975), 109.

[17] Cone, *God*, 124.

[18] Cone, *God*, 126.

Asian theologians not only use Christology as the means for understanding and articulating their faith but to connect to their neighbors of other faiths. In other words, not only is Jesus a means for us to relate to others in a particular way but a way for others to talk to us. The underlying assumption is that Christianity by itself is inadequate for understanding Christ. Others have wisdom about Christ that we are unable to see and in their speaking about Christ to us, we learn something about them as well. According to Japanese theologian Kosuke Koyama, "Our sense of the presence of God will be distorted if we fail to see God's reality in terms of our neighbour's reality."[19] Koyama believes we should turn to the cross as the means to understand Christ, because it is at the cross that we witness God's willingness to be foolish and weak to make God's self understandable.[20] It is that same mind-set that we must learn in order to make ourselves open to God. Koyama is concerned that we tend toward a crusading mind-set that turns away from the crucified Christ that points us toward a God that is beyond our understanding, to a resurrected pantocrator that is the one means to access God. The crusading mind "regards all who differ from us as 'nons'. We look at humanity as a whole, and then classify all those who are not Christians under the heading 'non-Christian.'"[21] As 'nons,' they are not people from whom we can receive any insight about God.

Asian theologians are contemptuous of that mind-set. Instead, they choose to understand what other faiths'

---

[19] Kosuke Koyama, *Waterbuffalo Theology* (Maryknoll, NY: 1974), 91.

[20] Kosuke Koyama, *No Handle on the Cross: An Asian Meditation on the Crucified Mind* (London: SCM Press, 1977), 86.

[21] Kosuke Koyama, *Fifty Meditations* (Maryknoll, NY: 1983), 124.

wisdom can teach us about Jesus. One such example is the Hindu concept of *avatar*. The idea of God becoming human is not unique to the Christian tradition. It is in fact what French anthropologist and ethnologist, and founder of structural mythology, Claude Lévi Strauss would call a bricolage piece.[22] These bricolage pieces or mythemes[23] show up in multiple cultures and religious systems and function in similar ways. When compared, they bring interesting wisdom to each other. It is in the comparison of bricolage pieces that the rich *variety and depth of meaning* in them comes out. In her book, *The Implied Spider*, historian of religion and Indologist, Wendy Doniger lays out a method of comparison. She believes theological texts and ideas act as lenses for one another. She echoes David Tracy's idea that we know others through the analogical imagination of similarity-in-difference. Tracy's ideas rest on Aristotle's idea that "to spot the similar in the dissimilar is the mark

---

22   Claude Lévi Strauss, *The Savage Mind*, trans. George Weidenfield and Nicholson Ltd. (Chicago: University of Chicago Press, 1962), 11. The use of bricoleur and bricolage in the space of myths and religions is worked out in Wendy Doniger's book, *The Implied Spider*, where she explains the bricoleur as a "rag and bones man" or fix-it man who collected old odds and ends like cloths and furniture and repurposed them. She contrasts this with patent-inventors who are creating an entirely new thing. The bricolage then is the bits and bobs the bricoleur—or storyteller—pulls out of his bag to cobble the story together. In so doing, the meaning/function that the bricolage piece had in its former use affects the new use of it. Somewhat like the repurposing of the window dressing by Scarlett O'Hara in *Gone with the Wind* (Wendy Doniger, *The Implied Spider: Politics and Theology in Myth* (New York: Columbia University Press, 1998), 137- 151).

23   Doniger, *Implied Spider*, 145.

of poetic genius." Tracy believes that it is through the reflection on similarity-through-difference that we are able to comprehend any relationship, whether it is "relationships within the self, the relationships of the self to other selves, to society, history, the cosmos."[24] Comparison, Doniger believes, requires having something in common to make sense of difference. Comparison is the engagement of the space between sameness and difference.[25]

The danger of focusing on difference, or setting oneself apart as different, is there is no point of connection with that to which one is relating and consequently no point from which to relate. Theology of Religions is the discipline that looks at the possible models for dealing with multiple faiths. Not surprisingly for Christians, how we understand Christ determines in great part which model we operate out of. When the uniqueness of Christ is overemphasized, we find ourselves operating in what Galvin D'Costa calls the Exclusivist model and which Paul Knitter categorizes as the Replacement and Acceptance models,[26] where faiths are viewed as so different from each other that they have no way of relating to each other.

Overemphasis on sameness on the other hand merges all into one, leaving nothing to compare and consequently nothing to relate to. Rather than the overemphasis of uniqueness where one is focused on difference, sameness

---

24 David Tracy, *The Analogical Imagination: Christian Theology and the Culture of Pluralism* (New York: Crossroad, 1981), 410.

25 Doniger, *Implied Spider*, 27–28.

26 Gavin D'Costa, *Theology and Religious Pluralism* (New York: Basil Blackwell, 1986). Paul Knitter, *Introducing Theologies of Religions* (Maryknoll: Orbis Books, 2002).

erases difference altogether. Theology of religions would call this the Inclusivist model (D'Costa) or Fulfillment model (Knitter) of dealing with other faiths. Doniger suggests that there is an ominousness to the focus on sameness as well. There is a power afforded to the one who defines how things are the same. The one with the ability to define has the power to make its understanding of a concept the ideal and render all other understandings as extensions or even pejorative versions of that ideal. Doniger uses the cases of racism and sexism to illustrate the point. The idea that mankind can be the arching descriptor for gender or the idea that "we are all human" overrides racial realities is a way to dismiss difference and falsely smooth over power dynamics and conflicts. This is not only problematic, it is oppressive.[27]

Similarity is the space where points of sameness can be used to make connections between ideas and people possible, while difference is recognized and makes the relationship between those ideas and people dynamic and interesting.[28] Unless one is a narcissist, relationship needs difference to give an other to relate to and sameness to relate through.

Mythemes like incarnation are excellent spaces to do the work of comparison of similarity-in-difference and in so doing see the relationship between faiths, which brings us back to incarnation themes in Hinduism through the concept of *avatar*. Hinduism actually mentions ten different incarnations or *avatars* of Vishnu: the dwarf, the fish, the

---

27   Wendy Doniger, *The Implied Spider: Politics and Theology in Myth* (New York Columbia University Press, 1998), 31–33.

28   Doniger, *Implied Spider,* 34–36.

boar, the tortoise, Krishna, Rama, Parashurama, Kalki, the Man-Lion, and even the Buddha. Not only do each of these incarnations have their own particular value and wisdom but they come through out time in different creaturely forms and even religious and cultural systems to aid the cosmos. This way of attending to this *avatar* bricolage piece helps the Hindu see incarnation wherever it may manifest, both in their own faith systems and in other faith systems like Buddhism and Christianity. They can understand the Buddha and Christ because they understand the function of Rama and Krishna and how they work.[29]

Doniger believes theological ideas act as lenses for one another. Mythemes like incarnation both compare and are amenable to comparison. According to the Hindu mystic and yogi, Sri Ramakrishna:

> It is one in the same *Avatar* that, having plunged into the ocean of life, rises up in one place and is known as Krishna and diving again rises in another place and is known as Christ.[30]

His disciple, Swami Vivekananda expands on this idea,

> The disciple thinks the Lord can manifest Himself only once. There lies the whole mistake. God manifests Himself to you in man. But throughout Nature, what happens once must have happened before, and must happen in the future. There is nothing in Nature, which

---

[29] Wendy Doniger, *The Hindus: An Alternative History* (New York: The Penguin Press, 2009), 473–493.

[30] Quoted by Max Muller, *Ramakrishna: His Life and Sayings*, Collected Works, vol. 15 (London: Longmans, Green & Co, 1900), 109.

> is not bound by law, and that means whatever happens once, must go on and must have been going on ... Let us therefore find God not only in Jesus of Nazareth but in all the great Ones that have preceded him, in all that came after him, and all that are yet to come. Our worship is unbounded and free. They are all manifestations of the same Infinite God.[31]

It is because they can recognize the bricolage of incarnation in their own faith tradition that they can also see it in Christ.

It must be noted that Sri Ramakrishna and Vivekananda fall into the proclivity of inclusivism and believe that the arching narrative of the Vedanta tradition is the means to explain incarnation and flatten out the unique vision in the incarnation of Christ, and for that matter even of Buddha, to suit the Vedantan narrative. Setting that aside, the recognition of the similar bricolage of incarnation in different times, places, and even different religions allows them space to compare them and learn what particular wisdom each manifestation brings. Consequently, they enlighten Christians to the wisdom Christ brings in a way we were not aware of before and open us to other manifestations of incarnation and their wisdom.

This underscores why we need a contextual, inculturated way of understanding incarnation. It is the way the particularity of that context and the incarnation manifested in it come to light. In the words of D. Preman Niles:

---

[31] *The Complete Works of Swami Vivekananda*, vol I, 5th ed. (Almora: Advaita Ashrama, 1931), xiii.

Is theology always a matter of Text to Context? Is it not also a matter of relating Context to Text so that the context may speak to the text? Is Asia only there to receive? Has it nothing to contribute? If it does, then theology can no longer be viewed as a monologue. It is a dialogue.[32]

The questions asked by Niles about the relationship of text and context can also be asked about Christ and context and similar conclusions are reached. It is not only Christ that illuminates context but context also illuminates Christ.

This way of thinking also highlights the abundant nature of God as God is willing to come to the world over and over again and in so doing brings new wisdom in multiple finite ways that are accessible to us. It makes sense that the gracious God we have a sense of in our Christian faith would try again and again in multiple ways to be accessible and relate to us.

This way of thinking requires us to critique the proclivity of Christians to equate uniqueness with singularity. For a reality to be unique, it does not have to be the only option. It is possible to bring a unique insight to a plurality of understandings. To put it another way: uniqueness is not the problem, singularity is.

Another space where comparative work has been done is between Christ and Buddha. R.S. Sugirtharajah lifts up the ideas of Indian philosopher and statesman Sarvepalli

---

[32] D. Permanent Niles, "The Word of God and the People of Asia," in *Understanding the Word: Essays in Honor of Bernhard W. Anderson,* Journal for the Study of the Old Testament, Supplement Series 37, eds. James T. Butler, Edgar W. Conrad, and Ben C. Ollenburger (Sheffield, England: JSOT Press, 1985), 283.

Radhakrishnan in this area.[33] Radhakrishnan points to the similarities in Buddha's and Christ's life narratives: the miraculous birth connected to a supernatural source, the temptations they faced, the selection and sending out of disciples to propagate their teachings, their revolt against the expression of the religion into which they were born, and even the quaking of the earth when both men died. These are only a few of the common themes between them. This makes them, in Radhakrishnan's words, "men of the same brotherhood."[34] Radhakrishnan also points to the ascetism in their teaching, an idea[35] also explored by Aloysius Pieris[36] as he works out the idea of voluntary poverty as a tool of liberation in his Buddhist homeland of Sri Lanka.

Japanese scholar of New Testament and Buddhist-Christian dialogue Seiichi Yagi[37] notes that both Christ and Buddha deal with the idea of the estranged ego that is infused with false value.

These points of similarity help highlight the differences between Buddha and Christ as a means to learn from them. Yagi notes that the way the two address the estranged ego differs. Buddha addresses the falseness of the ego itself. Jesus speaks about the false inflation, or perhaps false deflation, of the ego, of the ego masking what it was intended to be by God. Radhakrishnan notes that Buddha spoke

---

[33] R.S. Sugirtharajah, *Jesus in Asia* (Cambridge: Harvard University Press, 2018), 186–189.

[34] As quoted in Sugirtharajah, *Jesus in Asia,* 186.

[35] Sugirtharajah, *Jesus in Asia,* 187

[36] Aloysius Pieris, *Love Meets Wisdom: A Christian Experience of Buddhism* (Maryknoll: Orbis Books, 1988), 129–135.

[37] Seiichi Yagi, "Christ and Buddha" in *Asian Faces of Jesus,* ed. R.S. Sugirtharajah (Maryknoll: Orbis Books, 1993), 25–31.

about the suprapersonal spirit while Jesus spoke about the personal God.[38] Both Jesus and Buddha teach that there can be a redemptive wisdom that comes out of suffering. However, a dying savior that is a key example of that idea in Christianity is absent in Buddhism. Both agree that the world is a broken place, but Buddha's reasoning for it is false attachment, while for Jesus it is sin. It is here in the comparison of the differences within similar themes that we can gain insight. It is not surprising that these insights come from Asia, a context that is defined by a plurality of cultures and religions.

The issue is, how do we take these multiple contextual visions of Christology seriously in a manner that allows the insights of different understandings of incarnation to inform each other without merging them or choosing one as the universal. The means of doing that is conversation or dialogue. Dialogue, simply put, is the space where the conversation between particulars is possible.

Dialogue, as I am using the idea here, is a free-flowing conversation for the discovery of new knowledge and wisdom not only about others but about oneself in relationship with others. Gordon Kaufman puts forward a rationale for dialogue and describes it as "a way to understand our religiousness that can honour the integrity and meaning of each religious tradition *and yet open it* to appreciation of and reconciliation with others."[39]

Dialogue allows the real differences between people's insights and understanding the integrity they deserve. Rather

---

[38] Sugirtharajah, *Jesus in Asia*, 187.

[39] Gordon Kaufman, *God, Mystery, Diversity* (Minneapolis: Fortress Press, 1996), 191. Emphasis mine.

than overriding differences with a false sameness or over-emphasizing those differences, thereby making any connection between them impossible, it uses those differences as a resource of wisdom for all.

Raimon Panikkar in his work differentiates between what he calls the dialectical dialogue and dialogical dialogue.[40] Dialectical dialogue deals primarily with reasons, facts, and rational ways of understanding. It is about using dialogue to focus on a particular subject and make rational sense of it in a manner all the participants can agree on. It presumes that contradictions are not possible and ideas that do not fit the universal consensus of what is reasonable are abandoned for what is deemed rational. Its primary mode is debate and its goal is rational consensus. Panikkar also notes that dialectical dialogue "can be an instrument to power and can be a means to the will to power."[41] There is an asserting of one understanding of reason upon others with the end of overwhelming them and having them acquisce to one's own idea of what is rational.

Dialogical dialogue is, by contrast, a means of discovery. Like dialectical dialogue, it is based on a subject (in our case Christology) but its purpose is not to figure out the rational consistencies of what we believe that subject is about. Rather, our goal in a dialogical dialogue is to learn about the other persons who are in the dialogue, how they each understand the subject, how their understandings affect how we understand the subject, and what more we may discover

---

[40]   Raimon Panikkar, *The Intra-Religious Dialogue* (New York: Paulist Press, 1999), 23–40.

[41]   Panikkar, *Dialogue*, 31.

about it together.[42] Dialogical dialogue is more about what Panikkar calls the I-Thou-It relationship, where all three are dynamic critical components in the understanding of the whole and each of its parts. They only function in relation to each other.

> The I and Thou statements can never set the speaking subject aside; they cannot be substantives in the sense of being reified, cut off from the I and the thou and made into eternal immutable 'truths'. In the dialogue we are reminded constantly of our temporality, our contingency, our own constitutive limitations. Humility is not primarily a moral virtue but an ontological one; it is the awareness of the place of my ego, the truthfulness of accepting my real situation, namely, that I am a situated being, a vision's angle on the real, an existence.[43]

In this type of dialogue, a will to power will not allow the dialogue to take place.[44]

Kaufman deepens the idea that dialogue has a life of its own that is more than the sum total of those participating in it: "Sometimes in an exciting conversation of this sort, the participants are 'carried away' by the flow of the conversation itself, which has come to have a seeming intention of its own.... truth is perceived as a process of becoming, a reality that emerges (quite unexpectedly) in the course of conversation—a reality that, if the conversation continues, may (or may not) continue to break in upon the participants."[45]

---

42   Panikkar, *Dialogue*, 29–32.

43   Panikkar, *Dialogue*, 37.

44   Panikkar, *Dialogue*, 31.

45   Kaufman, *God*, 199.

Kaufman says the truth being sought after in such a dialogue or conversation is different from truth sought after in dialectical dialogue or what he calls truth in the modern sense. That kind of truth is truth as fact or truth "heavily influenced by scientific ideas ... a highly reflective, carefully argued metaphysical claim about ultimate reality."[46] The truth sought after in dialogical dialogue is what Kaufman calls premodern truth. That is, truth that is useful to bring about the fullness of life to human beings.[47] He is using the idea of fullness of life in a similar way to David Ford in his book, *Theology: A Short Introduction*. Ford explains that the root of the word for salvation (*soterios*) is health. Health should be understood in terms of all the dimensions of well-being including but not limited to: mental, economic, social, spiritual, environmental, and moral. In other words, salvation is concerned with the things that bring about human flourishing.[48] Truth, in the pre-modern sense, is the practical knowledge that brings about such flourishing.[49] Such truth may not be useful for all time, but it aids flourishing in the particular place in which it is meaningful. It is very much reflected in the raft metaphor used by the Buddha to describe truth. The raft is useful to cross the river but it is not to be clung to afterward.[50] It should be noted how contextual this definition of truth is. Truth is deeply connected to the context in which it is expressed and

---

46   Kaufman, *God*, 192.

47   Kaufman, *God*, 192.

48   David Ford, *Theology: A Short Introduction* (Oxford: Oxford University Press, 2013), 102.

49   Kaufman, *God*, 192.

50   Wapola Rahula, *What the Buddha Taught* (New York: Grove Press, 1974), 11–12.

how useful it is to the fullness of life in that place. It is this very kind of truth that Christology as a theology of incarnation reveals and dialogical dialogue empowers.

Kenneth Cracknell refers to the idea of pilgrimage, which he picks up from the World Council of Churches Guidelines for Interfaith dialogue.[51] Pilgrimage is a useful word as it puts us on a path toward a particular spiritual end. On the way we meet other people on their own journeys. We journey together for a time and share the wisdom we have gained from our particular travels and they share the wisdom from theirs. Sometimes their journey is so compelling we decide to follow their pilgrimage path. Sometimes the wisdom of their journey just makes us wiser on our own and we can do the same for them. The journeys are not the same, nor are the ends that we are trying to reach, but we can still exchange wisdom as we travel along our particular pathways. The situation is very much like backpackers traveling through Europe. We may not be going to the same place but we may journey together for a while and share wisdom we have gained on our way, pleasant places we have rested, and share food and toiletries we have picked up. How we use the wisdom others share with us might be different from how they use it themselves. For example, someone may have given us shampoo that we use, and need, as body wash!

To access such truth and wisdom requires a trust of one's conversation partners as exactly that, partners in the unearthing and perception of truth that without them would not come into being. This is truth that cannot be found in

---

[51] Kenneth Cracknel, *In Good and Generous Faith* (Cleveland: The Pilgrim Press, 2005), 136–139.

competition but requires participation, reliance, and trust. Panikkar explains this beautifully when he says, "I trust the other not out of an ethical principle (because it is good) or an epistemological one (because I recognise that it is intelligent to do so), but because I have discovered (experienced) the *'thou'* as the counterpart of the I, as belonging *to* the I (and not as not-I). I trust the partner's understanding and self-understanding because I do not start out by putting ego as the foundation of everything …. I find in his actual presence something irreducible to my ego and yet not belonging to a nonego."[52]

Kaufman and Panikkar both understand dialogue as an act we participate in. The power of it goes deeper when we understand it as a state of being. The idea here is to move from dialogical dialogue to dialogical existence. Dialogue is not only a praxis but an ontological state. It echoes what we discussed in the previous chapter about God as a relational being. Relationship is not merely what God does but what God is. Being dialogical is about being relational. God then is the ultimate dialogical being within Godself and the cosmos is the truth that emerges out of that dialogue. Our very existence is dialogical. Dialogue describes our very nature. As Panikkar puts it, "The anthropological assumption is that Man is not an individual but a person, that is, a set of relationships."[53] We are a summation of the dialogues we are part of. We are "fields of interaction where the real has been woven or striped by means of all the complexity of

---

[52] Panikkar, *Dialogue*, 38.

[53] Panikkar, *Dialogue*, 24.

reality ... [we] are knots in the continuous weaving of the net of reality."[54]

Into this conversation, Kwok Pui Lan adds a cautionary note. Dialogue is not without power dynamics because not all of the partners have equal space to express themselves, nor are all the partners, because of their place of privilege, able or willing to take the importance of all voices seriously. As she says, "It should be pointed out that in our post-colonial world, all the voices are not equal and some cultures have dominated centre stage, with the power to push the rest to the periphery."[55]

For dialogue to pursue truth in the pre-modern sense as Kaufman describes it, as being about the flourishing of life, it must be liberative. This requires that everyone is allowed to speak and that all voices in the conversation are truly heard without one voice dominating and overriding the center stage. Aloysius Pieris states that the announcement of the liberative act of God is one that humanizes a dehumanized world and has been recognized by people pushed to the margins, othered, and dismissed. These are the spaces where people of the Third World both economically and theologically exist. Interestingly, he notes that the Third World is also the space where voices of people of other faiths can be heard: "The irruption of the Third world is also the irruption of the non-Christian world. The vast majority of God's poor perceive their ultimate concern and symbolise their struggle for liberation in the idiom of non-Christian religions and cultures. Therefore, a theology

---

[54] Panikkar, *Dialogue*, 39.

[55] Kwok Pui-Lan, *Postcolonial Imagination and Feminist Theology* (Louisville: Westminster John Knox Press, 2005), 42.

that does not speak to this non-Christian peoplehood is an esoteric luxury of a Christian minority. Hence, we need a theology of religions [including a Christology] that will explain the existing boundaries of orthodoxy as we enter into the liberative streams of other religions and cultures."[56]

Notice the close link being made by Kaufman and Pieris between the concept of salvation and liberation. Indian theologian M. M. Thomas describes it more succinctly by saying salvation is humanization taken to its eschatological conclusion.[57] The forces that dehumanize the world are felt most deeply at the margins, the irruption that Pieris is talking about is the humanizing work of God in, through, and with the marginalized in their particular location. The problem with power is it privileges the central voice over all others. It decontextualizes this central voice and uses it to override all other voices, silencing those who do not have the power to overcome it. Those voices that are silenced are those at the margins, cutting us off from the liberative and therefore salvific insights they bring. To put it another way: the ability to hear the voices hereunto ignored is not only a just and good thing to do, but a necessary thing to do to be able to have a fuller understanding of the self, the other, and the divine for the flourishing of life.

Christology is the Christian's way to always pay attention to context and make space for those at the margins. Bishop

---

56   Aloysius Pieris, *An Asian Theology of Liberation* (Edinburgh: T & T Clark, 1988), 87.

57   M.M. Thomas, *Salvation and Humanisation: Some Crucial Issues of the Theology of Mission in Contemporary India* (Madras: Christian Literature Society, 1971), 18.

V.S. Azariah put this eloquently in his speech to the 1910 World Mission Conference in Edinburgh when he said:

> The exceeding riches of the glory of Christ can be fully realised not by the Englishman, the American and the Continental alone, nor by the Japanese, the Chinese and the Indian by themselves—but by working together, worshipping together, and learning together the Perfect Image of our Lord and Christ. It is only "with all the Saints" that we can "comprehend the love of Christ which passeth knowledge, that we might be filled with all the fullness of God." This will be possible only from spiritual friendships between two races. We ought to be willing to learn from one another and to help one another. [58]

This kind of intra-Christian conversation not only deepens our own understanding of Christ but allows us to participate in wider interfaith conversations. Many other faiths have interpreted and appropriated Christ and Christian ideas in their own way. Understanding how they have done so gives us a path into the way they understand who they are and how they understand God and the world. It also provides a unique opportunity to see Christ anew through their eyes and enrich our thinking about Christ even further. This plurality in experiencing Christ moves us away from attempts to construct an overarching Christology. Rather, these voices call us into an ongoing conversation among many Christologies, each bringing its own gifts to an intra-Christian and interfaith dialogue.

---

[58] "The Problem of Co-operation between Foreign and Native Workers," in *World Missionary Conference 1910 Edinburgh: The History and Records of the Conference*, vol. 9 (Edinburgh & London: Oliphant, Anderson & Ferrier, 1910), 315.

CHAPTER 3

HOLY SPIRIT IN A PLURALISTIC WORLD

Language not only describes reality, it actually creates it. According to David Tracy, we do not experience or comprehend something and then put words to it. We actually understand in and through the languages available to us.[1] Language shapes meaning itself. For those of us who have the gift to exist and express ourselves in multiple languages, we have seen how the world embodies differently in different languages. In the same manner, Christ is the particular language through which Christians make meaning. The question that arises is: how do we communicate across languages? To put it another way: how do we in our particularity understand and seek to be understood by others who see and make sense of the world in different languages? More importantly, how do we do it as true dialogue partners that can share, hear, transform, and be transformed by our dialogue partners for whom Christological language is not

---

[1]	David Tracy, *Plurality and Ambiguity: Hermeneutics, Religion, Hope* (San Francisco: Harper & Row, 1987), 48.

their means of perceiving the world. The Christian doctrine that is the most helpful in this regard is the Holy Spirit.

It is not altogether surprising that one of the prominent biblical texts addressing the Holy Spirit focuses on communication and language. The Pentecost narrative in Acts 2:5-11 is about all the nations of what could be considered the biblically known (Mediterranean) world.[2] The Spirit descended upon all of them and they could understand what the gathered disciples were saying in their own languages.[3] In their own language is another way of saying mother tongue, which is not only the language you learned as a child but the language with which you were nursed, the language with which meaning-making began. It was the first pattern system out of which our reality emerged and therefore holds an emotionally formative place in our being. I remember some years ago when theologian and hymnist Thomas Thangaraj came to my American-English speaking church in the Midwest to lead World Communion Sunday. He led most of the service in English, the language both of us live and function in with great dexterity. I confess that English is actually my first language. Suddenly, when he was to speak the words of institution for the Lord's Supper, he switched to our mother tongue, Tamil. While Tamil is not a language I move in with great fluidity, I found myself thrown into a space of deeper meaning. The language of the sacrament, that I have heard so often in my first language,

---

2   Amos Yong, *Pneumatology and the Christian Buddhist Dialogue: Does the Spirit Blow through the Middle Way?* (Leiden: Brill, 2012), 13.

3   D. Preman Niles, "Toward the Fullness of Life," *International Review of Mission* 491 (October 2002): 477.

suddenly came to me in the language that surrounded me at my birth and out of which I first experienced the world. This central sacrament, meant to nurture the faith, was given to me in the actual language in which I was nurtured. I believe I was much like those present at that first Pentecost moment, who were hearing God's message in their own language. It hit my heart and brought me to tears and I understood in a completely new way what is meant when we say communion is sacramental and transformative.

This makes Pentecost a powerful metaphor to explain the Holy Spirit. If indeed language makes meaning, the meaning-making in one language is being translated by the Holy Spirit to another meaning-making reality in a manner that makes sense in that other reality.

The Holy Spirit is an equal part of the Trinity. It is equally in and through every part of the cosmos. Therefore, the Spirit not only serves to make the particularity of Christ understandable to *others* in their particularity, but the Spirit, because of its connections to others in their particularity, can also connect them to *us* in ways that make sense and enrich us in our particularity. D. Preman Niles states, "Acts 2 does not abrogate plurality as a divisive human condition, but rather affirms it as an enriching of one another in a receptive plurality."[4]

The Holy Spirit functions as a great translator between particularities, making communication within the plurality possible. As the translator, the Spirit is in fact the source that makes dialogue possible because it makes communication possible and does it in a non-imperialistic way.

---

[4]   Niles, *Fullness of Life*, 477.

Amos Yong states that "a pneumatological approach to the interreligious dialogue informed by the Day of Pentecost narrative will invite the voices of those in other faiths to be sounded in all their particularity."[5] All the languages of meaning-making can hear and be heard by each other in a manner that enriches them all without the colonial need to make them one.

What needs to be pointed out, and which Amos Yong does well, is that Pentecost is not the point where the Holy Spirit enters the biblical narrative. Rather the Spirit has always been present in the story, even before Genesis.

Before creation, there was chaos. Understanding chaos is necessary for understanding creation and the divine's relationship to both. James Huchingson states that chaos is as critical to understanding anything and everything as are the concepts of God and being. The idea of chaos gives a patina to how things arise, perish, and how they persist.[6]

Descriptions of chaos in classical Christian thought, Huchingson reminds us, tend to portray it in negative terms. The turbulent primordial ooze is depicted as confusing and destructive, always waiting to overwhelm us and disintegrate our creative (read good) state.[7] However, that is but one aspect of chaos. It also is abundant with creative possibility. Huchingson describes this complex nature well when he says, "(primordial chaos) exhibits aspects of emptiness, abysmal depth, devouring menace, and violent

---

5   Yong, *Pneumatology*, 15.

6   James E. Huchingson, *Pandemonium Tremendum: Chaos and Mystery in the Life of God* (Cleveland: The Pilgrim Press, 2001), 102.

7   Huchingson, *Pandemonium*, 96–99.

agitation or confusion. And yet, there are elements of potentiality, of source and power, not only for obliteration but also for birth. The chaos is not static but clearly dynamic in a threatening and productive way. While it hides and resists creation by guarding its dark depths, its very energy is potentially available to drive the creation's ordering processes."[8]

The *Matsya Purana*[9] provides a helpful story that illuminates these complex ideas. In this story, the great sage Markandeya, during the interval of the dissolving and recreation of the universe, enters the body of the god Vishnu as he sleeps and dreams of what the recreated universe should be while reclining on the primordial sea of chaos. By accident, the sage falls into the sea and begins to drown. He panics and pulls himself out back into the body of Vishnu and the vision of order that Vishnu is dreaming. Markandeya is wet and moist with the chaos' reality. As he sits there in the clear order of the vision, he dries out and becomes brittle. He yearns for the moistness of the chaos and tips himself back into it. This time he can enjoy the moist overwhelming reality of the chaos, but he still cannot breathe. So he pulls himself back into the body to get air and perspective. Back and forth he goes, thriving between the two realities. Human beings are like that. We are part of the moist chaos of plurality, but we need the dry air of comprehension to negotiate it and find our place in it. If

---

[8]   Huchingson, *Pandemonium*, 101.

[9]   *Matsya Purana* CLXVII, 13–66. See H Zimmer's rendering of this story in his *Myths and Symbols in the Art and Civilization of India* as summarized in: Lakshman Wickremesinghe, "Living in Christ with People," *CTC Bulletin* 5, no. 1–2 (April–August, 1984).

we spend too much time in the moist chaotic mystery, we drown. If we spend too much time in the clear air of order, we become dry and brittle. We need to negotiate the space between chaos and the structures of creation. This vision of creation describes chaos in a more positive way. Rather than standing in menacing opposition to creation waiting to deconstruct it, chaos becomes the source of creation that not only provides the potential for it but keeps creation dynamic, flexible, and viable.

The difficulty with the concept of chaos is that it defies definition. Chaos is not the opposite of order. Chaos confuses and interrupts order, giving space for new possibilities and connections within creation. Huchingson calls chaos "the annihilation or obliteration of order, pattern, and expectable process."[10] He actually goes on further to call chaos anarchy, a continuum of disordered states that are acausal, indeterminate, and ungoverned by any organizing principle.[11] It is no wonder that, as he eloquently puts it, "chaos eludes all attempts at analysis and is amenable primarily to the poetic imagination."[12]

The reason chaos eludes analysis is because it is pure plurality that cannot be reduced to patterns that can in turn be described. Chaos, Huchingson explains, "is an infinite field of variety (plurality), of complete indeterminateness filled with potency, the source of all created things."[13] This is an apt description of the primordial sea of chaos that Markandeya falls into in the *Matsya Purana*. The plurality

---

[10]   Huchingson, *Pandemonium*, 98.

[11]   Huchingson, *Pandemonium*, 97–98.

[12]   Huchingson, *Pandemonium*, 97–98.

[13]   Huchingson, *Pandemonium*, 105.

seen here is one where everything "is not yet limited by anything other than its own disconnectedness, detail, grain, and texture."[14] Chaos holds the potential for infinite possibilities of relationships, some of which can be made actual in creation.

It is not surprising that this idea would invoke panic, confusion, and fear as it did for Markandeya as he fell into the sea of chaos where he could not breathe. He, as a finite mortal creature, cannot be anything but overwhelmed by it. But it must not be forgotten that Vishnu floats on that sea, dreaming new patterns of relationships out of the infinite possibilities provided by the chaotic sea. Also, Markandeya needs that chaotic variety to keep all the potential connections viable and himself flexible and therefore truly alive.

The Genesis story is interpreted in classical theology to juxtapose chaos with creation rather than seeing the two as complementary. This sells the Genesis story short. Genesis also sees chaos as the source of creative possibility. Hong Kong Chinese scholar Archie Lee reminds us that Genesis 1 is accepted by most scholars to have its roots in Babylonian creation stories. The exilic community, through the voice of the priestly tradition, takes over the basic tale from its captors and repurposes it to show God's purposeful hand in guiding Israel.[15] The Babylonian creation myth, the *Emuma Elish*, states, "When on high the heavens had not yet been named ... then the gods were created in their midst."[16] Lee

---

14 Huchingson, *Pandemonium,* 104–105.

15 Archie Chi-Chung Lee, "Creation Narratives and the Movement of the Spirit," from *Doing Theology with the Spirit's Movement in Asia* (Singapore: ATESEA, 1991), 23.

16 Lee, *Creation Narratives,* 18.

points out that creation in this way of telling the story presupposes a preexisting chaos out of which everything, even the gods, emerges. This background information colors the creation myth in Genesis. There is the idea of a pre-creation chaos out of which God makes a creative order.[17] Huchingson describes the potentiality found in chaos in the following manner:

> The earth, that is, the world in its totality (including, presumably, the heavens as well), has no form or presence. Still, there remains an unspoken anticipation, prepared for by the announcement in (Genesis) verse 1, that this state of desolation is about to change, that the earth, merely a gleam in the eye of God, is *as yet* without form and void.[18]

Amos Yong calls for a pneumatological theology of creation.[19] To do that, it is necessary to widen the focus of creation to include the time before creation. Genesis focuses on the creation and God as the creator. But what can be said about the time before the creation and the formless chaotic void and darkness that covered the face of the deep? This is the dominion of the Holy Spirit. The Holy Spirit hovers over the raw chaotic material out of which the relationships that form creation are made. Huchingson argues that chaos is not only the dominion over which the Holy Spirit hovers, but the Spirit actually dwells within it. Huchingson likens the Holy Spirit in chaos to the Leviathan lurking, stalking, and disturbing the churning waters from within. He describes the dominion of the Holy Spirit over chaos as the

---

17   Lee, *Creation Narratives*, 18.

18   Huchingson, *Pandemonium*, 100.

19   Yong, *Pneumatology*, 37.

ruach, a howling cyclonic wind that echoes the turbulence that it hovers over.[20] The Spirit does not calm it and soothe it or make order of it, but glories in it and empowers it.

The Spirit also shows up at the end of the creation narrative in Genesis 1:30 and 2:7, where it breathes the gift of life into creatures.[21] This takes the very nature of chaos, of which the Holy Spirit is a part, and breathes it into the creative process. It is that breath that gives the creation life. It honors radical particularity and resists any move to overlook and override it for the sake of the creative process. The Spirit also keeps the creative patterns from becoming dry and brittle, in other words, lifeless. It disrupts the patterns of creation with other particularities to make more potential relationships possible. In other words, the Holy Spirit brings chaos into and through the creation process, keeping it vibrant and dynamic and full of possibilities.

In this way, it resists the colonizing process. In the colonizing process, one single pattern of relationship is used to override other possibilities of relationship that an honoring of difference allows. This is done in the name of order. The Holy Spirit allows the disruption of order with particularity. This may be why there is an impulse to subsume the Holy Spirit to a more orderly idea like the Creator, the Church or, as is often the case in Christianity, to Christ. But to really experience the Holy Spirit, it needs to be encountered on its own terms.

This is actually a very yin-yang way of coming at these ideas. Creation and chaos are not drawn in opposition to each other or even really in dialectic relationship with each

---

20   Huchingson, *Pandemonium*, 100–101.
21   Yong, *Pneumatology*, 37.

other, but in symbiotic relationship. In a yin-yang way of thinking, seeming opposites are actually just a part of a larger whole and they need each other.[22] The particular elements of chaos need creation to bring them into actual relationship with each other and creation needs the particularity of chaos to provide the elements for relationship and keep it vibrant. They depend on each other and you cannot have one without the other. The Spirit ties them together and uses one to fulfill the possibility of the other.

A biblical text that could help us have a healthier understanding of chaos and plurality, as well as God's intention for it, and perhaps even help us resist the colonizing impulse to move to a single dominant narrative, is the story of the Tower of Babel in Genesis 11:1–9. This text has two clear movements: humanity's movement inward and God's pushing them outward. It is the interpretation of these movements that makes the text interesting. The dominant tradition of interpretation views humanity's movement inward as sinful hubris in the face of God. God's response is thus interpreted as punishing or even cursing humanity with plurality. Even Gerhard Von Rad, who reads the text with a more generous eye, sees God's act as punitive, indeed even preventive.[23] Underpinning this interpretation is the assumption that the ideal state of humanity is the assumed prior state of humanity: with "one language and the same

---

[22] Jung Young Lee, "The Ying-Yang Way of Thinking," in *Asian Christian Theology: Emerging Themes*, ed. Douglas J. Elwood (Philadelphia: The Westminster Press, 1980), 81–88.

[23] Gerhard Von Rad, *Genesis: A Commentary* (Philadelphia: Westminster Press, 1972), 149.

words," and the divine punishment was the destruction of that state.

An alternative interpretation, using a lens of pluralism, is that of Bernard W. Anderson. Anderson asserts that the importance of the Tower of Babel story lies in its addressing of our common humanity as creatures of God and of pluralism as the Creator's purpose. He draws attention to three points that are worth noting: 1. This pericope is a well-structured literary unit and refers to nothing before it or after it. 2. The interpretation of this pericope has not always been that God's scattering of humanity is a punishment. Josephus and John Calvin as well as several other rabbinic interpreters have understood it as a benediction that flowed from God. 3. A proper interpretation of the pericope would be to see it in the context of the primeval history covered in Gen 1–11 as a part of the whole of human history and God's desire for humanity. The desire of God for humanity is given in Genesis 1:28—"God blessed them and said to them, 'Be fruitful and multiply and fill the earth and subdue it.'" Leaving aside all the complications attached to "subduing," the main point of the blessing is the fruitfulness in multiplying and filling the earth (land) that was in danger of being subverted at Babel. So, God came down and confused their language and scattered them over the face of the earth and they left off building the city and returned to God's original intention of filling the earth.[24]

Thickening this discussion, Nestor Miguez suggests that Genesis 11:1–9 refers back to Genesis 10:8–12. Seen in this manner, the characters referred to in Genesis 11 are not all

---

[24] Bernhard W. Anderson, "Unity and Diversity in God's Creation," *Currents in Theology and Mission* 5, no.2 (April, 1978): 71–80.

of humanity but a particular group of people from the Table of Nations: Nimrod and his followers. This is a man who has left his father Cush's home and occupies lands "not of his family," first in Shinar and then Assyria.[25] Thus, Babel may be interpreted as a story not of human beings' hubris in relationship with God but in relationship with each other. The tower, Miguez argues, is not a means to reach God but a means of keeping watch over the earth.[26] In response, God comes down and performs a liberative act by confusing the language of the conqueror so that this occupation is no longer possible. This, he states, is a blessing for the people who were conquered. The people who were under the hegemonic project of the people "with the same language" are released—allowing their own languages and cultures to be expressed again. God, according to Miguez, does not come down to punish; God can punish from anywhere. Instead, God descends to join people in order to overcome oppression.[27] This is a God who champions plurality because it is an act of liberation and therefore, blessing.

When seen in this way, the idea of "one language and the same words" looks much less ideal and actually far more oppressive. If you think about the idea of one language, a lingua franca so to speak, it is not just a dominant common language that people with different native languages use to

---

[25] Miguez points out that Cush is traditionally placed in Africa, south of Egypt or south of the Arabian Peninsula. Nester Miguez, "A Comparative Bible Study of Genesis 10–11:9: An Approach from Argentina" in *Scripture, Community, and Mission*, ed. Philip L. Wickeri (Hong Kong: Christian Conference of Asia & World Council of Churches, 2003), 158–9.

[26] Miguez, "Comparative Bible Study," 159–160.

[27] Miguez, "Comparative Bible Study," 160–1.

communicate; it was also the language of commerce and the court and therefore the language of power. Returning to David Tracy's idea that language creates meaning, the common language makes a unity by overriding all other possibilities of meaning-making. In so doing, it silences the languages not in power. Monica Melanchthon asks,

> Is it possible for the common language here to be deemed as the language of the oppressor? Subjugated communities often internalise the language, the symbol, and metaphor of the oppressor and begin to believe that it is appropriate or proper language, thereby denying themselves the ability to speak in their own language.[28]

Nestor Miguez uses the example of the Qom people of Argentina to bring this point to life. He shows how the language of conversion found in 2 Corinthians 5:17 about being "new creations in Christ, where things of old are put away" has caused the silencing of the Qom people. "Since more than 90 percent of the Qom people were christianized in this kind of message," he writes, "cultural identity, the people's organization and even the native language is endangered."[29] Through this so-called unifying religion, culture, and language, the very means of meaning-making and experiencing the world has been colonized and less powerful means have been silenced.

The problem with embracing all these "languages" is that they are confusing to negotiate. We cannot understand one

---

[28] Monica Jyotsna Melanchthon, "A Dalit Reading of Genesis 10-11:9," in *Scripture, Community, and Mission,* ed. Philip L. Wickeri (Hong Kong: Christian Conference of Asia & World Council of Churches, 2003), 177.

[29] Miguez, "Comparative Bible Study," 153.

another. We are Markandeya in the sea of chaos, moist with possibility but unable to breathe.

Pentecost, and the Holy Spirit's work in it, becomes the Christian response to negotiating all of these languages. In Acts 2:5-11, the problems of confusion and chaos are not overcome by the creation of "one language with the same words," but through the honoring of all languages in their own words as the Holy Spirit creates connections by forming lines of comprehension between them.

The Holy Spirit becomes the great translator that honors each language and the precious perceptions it brings and makes it accessible to other perceptions by making it understandable in those other languages. In this way, the Holy Spirit becomes a force for liberation and transformation. It breaks the dominance of a single powerful voice and allows the vulnerable voices to be heard and the wisdom of their insights to enrich the whole. Ironically, by being broken in this way, the dominant voice becomes a single voice bringing its particular wisdom among other voices, a capacity that it loses with its need to be the voice for all.

Stanley Samartha describes four characteristics of the Spirit.[30] The first is that the Spirit is free, full of spontaneity, and unpredictability. The second is that the Spirit is boundless. The Spirit that hovers over and works through the primordial chaos knows no limits. The third is that it has the power to create new relationships. The fourth characteristic is connected to the third and explains why the Holy Spirit is a liberative aspect of the divine. To make new relationships possible, the Holy Spirit must break down old oppressive

---

[30] Stanley J. Samartha, "The Holy Spirit and People of Other Faiths," *The Ecumenical Review* 42, no. 3–4 (July–Oct, 1990): 250–263.

structures: "It is the Spirit who provides inspiration, energy, and power to humble folk to rise up in righteous anger against tyranny, oppression, and injustice in society. As the Giver of Life, it is the Spirit who moves them to demand fullness of life, freedom, self-respect, and dignity."[31] It is also the same Spirit that empowers them, that makes it possible for them to be heard, and share their voice and vision in the larger conversation. It is, in fact, through the Holy Spirit that the liberative power of plurality comes to fruition.

---

[31]   Samartha, "The Holy Spirit," 258.

CHAPTER 4

THE HUMAN BEING AS A DIALOGICAL CREATURE

Christianity makes three claims about human beings: we are made in the image of God, we are finite beings, and we are broken.

To say we are made in the image of God is to say we are like God but in a finite fashion. In chapter one, we explored the attributes of God that help us take pluralism seriously: mystery and relationality. Human beings have both those attributes in finite ways. We are complex and mysterious beings.

Gordon Kaufman describes human beings as bio-historical beings. By this, he means to understand human beings as a complex set of relationships that include both the specific environmental and historical-cultural frameworks that have shaped them over thousands of generations.[1] In other words, a human being is shaped by environment and context.

---

[1]   Gordon Kaufman, *God, Mystery, Diversity: Christian Theology in a Pluralistic World* (Minneapolis: Fortress Press, 1996), 74.

This is not a universal understanding of human, but a particular and relational one that focuses on how a human is affected by and affects its particular relation to the earth and the varied sociocultural patterns throughout its particular history. We are relational beings. Kristin Johnston Largen asserts, "Human beings *are* relationships: that is, human identity—both individually and communally—comes into being only in and through the myriad network of relationships that create us."[2] Eleazer Fernandez echoes this sentiment when he states, "relationship is constitutive of who we are and what we can become."[3]

This also makes us complex, mysterious beings. The dynamic nature of every part of the networks of relationships we are shaped by makes us defy simple comprehension. Every new relationship we are exposed to makes us more mysterious. Our relationships not only change us, they complicate our identity further. I live in the hyphens of my identity as a South Indian American with strong influences from Southeast Asia and Far East Asia, not to mention being a child of the British Commonwealth. I have been raised in the Christian tradition, but that Christianity is deeply flavored by the Hinduism and Buddhism that are also essential parts of the environments that shape me. Mine is a complex identity that is constantly shifting due to the dynamic connections that have molded me and the many other connections that can and will become a part of

---

[2]   Kristin Johnston Largen, *Finding God Among Our Neighbors: An Interfaith Systematic Theology* (Minneapolis: Fortress Press, 2013), 188.

[3]   Eleazar S. Fernandez, *Reimagining the Human: Theological Anthropology in Response to Systemic Evil* (St. Louis: Chalice Press, 2004), 187.

me. I am not alone in this kind of reality; all human beings are complex intersections of shifting connections.

Both Kaufman and Fernandez take this idea further by noting that we are not made only through our relationships with God, human beings, and human structures, but also our relationships with the whole earth, the cosmos, and all that is in it. Kaufman uses his idea of the biological in biohistorical to suggest that we are shaped by the whole biological environment we are surrounded by and not just the sociocultural one.[4] Fernandez states forthrightly that insights from ecology make it clear that we need to recenter the human being because our model now is "not congruent with the web of life."[5] Such a recentered human being "is not the centre or apex of creation but a vital participant within the cosmic symphony."[6] Such a world view, he believes, would keep us from being so anthropocentric where we use the world as a discardable stepping stone to something better and beyond. He describes the ideal human being as one who is connected to the whole earth as a participant, not a central axis. He also believes that human beings cannot be conceived in pure static categories. The ideal human being is one who relates, and does so dynamically and flexibly, able to move and change with all that it encounters. He asserts that human beings need to be aware "that identities are dynamic and changing, and that identities need not be conceived in purist either-or categories. In our highly globalized world, it is more adequate to speak of 'both-and' or 'in-both' identities because people

---

4   Kaufman, *God*, 77–78.

5   Fernandez, *Reimagining*, 190.

6   Fernandez, *Reimagining*, 190.

assume multiple identities … The new society is inhabited by human beings who are experiencing liberation from the crucifying norm of pure identity."[7] This is why trying to find a person who is Asian enough to be "really" Asian, Christian enough to be "really" Christian or American enough to be "truly" American is an exercise in futility. When we see that human beings are complex intersections of shifting connections, the idea of a pure identity is revealed to be a fallacy.

To fully embrace our complex identities as true images of God, Fernandez believes we need to see the importance of difference. It is in the honoring of difference and relating through it that truly healthy humanity thrives. The problem of universals as they have been conceived is that they see difference as problems that need to be neutralized or overlooked to focus on similarities so that we can create a false sameness. Wendy Doniger in her article, "Myths and Methods in the Dark," talks about the overemphasis on sameness.

> The problem of the same and the different has become a major tension within the field of comparative mythology [or comparative religion, comparative anthropology or of any kind of comparative work], in which theories that emphasize the identity of two variants of a story and ignore their differences are regarded as amounting to 'a night in which all cows are black.' The texts themselves, the stories, shine light on this same question from a different direction, when they present masquerades in which different women (the sexist argument) or different people of another culture (the racist argument) appear to be alike in the night, or in the dark,

---

7   Fernandez, *Reimagining*, 203.

or in bed—just like those black cows (or as they often become, gray cats).[8]

The problem with explaining away difference with the "all the same in the dark" attitude is that it squeezes everything into a false sameness by way of a meta-framework of one's own devising. It should be noted that the one doing the devising is the one with the *power* to do so, hence Doniger's comment about sexism, racism, and, one could add, other oppressive mindsets. That said, an overemphasis on difference makes relationship impossible, leading to the common, yet false, idiom "good fences make good neighbours!"

Fernandez calls for "being-in-difference." He believes difference is the very heart of our ontology. It is the principle of our existence. The existence of difference is not our problem; our attitude toward it is. Rather than negating difference or seeing it as an obstacle to relationship, we need to find ways to relate through it to "promote greater wellbeing."[9]

In a similar vein, Preman Niles cites a tongue-in-check exegesis of Genesis 11 by Victor Premsagar: "God was so bored with looking at one people and listening to one language that, using as an excuse the thwarting of a human attempt to reach God, God came down and changed them into different races with different languages. Plurality is what God wanted!"[10] Niles asserts that what was implied in

---

[8] Wendy Doniger, "Myths and Methods in the Dark," *The Journal of Religion* 76, no. 4 (Oct. 1996): 531.

[9] Fernandez, *Reimagining*, 202–203.

[10] As cited in D. Preman Niles, *The Lotus and the Sun* (Barton: Barton Books, 2013), 3.

this humorous reading of the Genesis text is a salient truth. Plurality is God's desire. Seeing it as a problem that needs fixing is the mistake that leads us away from God's intention and causes us to sin and create the webs of sinfulness that trap us.[11]

The two Christian ideas that help us pay attention to plurality and relate through it are Christ and the Holy Spirit. In a fully Trinitarian understanding, being made in the image of God means we are also made in the image of Christ and the Holy Spirit as well.

Christ is the finite expression of the infinite God and in so being, Christ shows us how to be finite. In chapter 2, we looked at how through the incarnation Christ becomes embodied in a particular time and place. He becomes a particular biohistorical being. The best way to understand Christ is by understanding how he would make sense in different biohistorical situations and then figure out how each situation enriches and can be enriched by others.

Unfortunately, what we have done with Christology we have also done with anthropology. We have taken what was intended to be concepts that focus on finiteness and have made them universal. We have taken God embodied in a particular biohistorical moment and used it to speak about all times and places without regard to their very own biohistorical particularity. Christ's incarnation is overridden by the Cosmic Christ. In the same manner, theological anthropology, which is about creatures made as finite versions of God, is addressed in universalistic terms that override its finiteness.

---

[11]   Niles, *Lotus*, 3.

On the other side, the problem with overemphasis on the finite particularity of the biohistorical creatures is getting trapped in identity politics. We get caught in the silos of our particularity and fail to relate beyond them. It is from these silos that we create the fallacy of pure identities, of what is "real" Asian, "real" Christianity, "true" American, and so forth. Any deviation from these identity silos is deemed not good enough to be part of these identities. It is the Holy Spirit that becomes the aid and example in the process of overcoming stagnation in silos and that creates relationships between them. As seen in the Pentecost story, which we explored in chapter 3, the Holy Spirit creates connections across silos, allowing cross-fertilization for the enrichment of each and the multiplication of ways of being not yet realized. It is the Spirit that creates the hyphens and the opportunities to live within them.

What does it mean that we are created in the image of the Spirit? The Spirit is the Breath of Life, breathed by God into the human being to bring it to life. In other words, the human being is literally infused with the Holy Spirit and so has its characteristics. Indeed, this is true of the whole creation.

Amos Yong says that when we look at all of creation through the lens of the Holy Spirit's presence, three ideas come into focus. First, it is in the web of relationships that God is present, and that web is made and maintained by the Spirit.[12] Second, creatures' distinctiveness is shaped by all the relationships they are a part of and in turn they shape all of those relationships in a dynamic ebb and flow.

---

[12] Amos Yong, *Pneumatology and Christian-Buddhist Dialogue: Does the Spirit Blow through the Middle Way?* (Leiden: Brill, 2012), 56.

As he puts it, "all creaturely realities, from particular things to whole environments and everything in between, are constituted by various parts or systems even as higher level environments are able to exert causal influence on lower level entities through feedback loops."[13] Third, the Spirit is in and through every distinct part of Creation and every connection between entities.[14] Therefore, as the human being participates in relationships through its finite distinctiveness, it embodies its *imago dei* as one made in the image of the Spirit. As we have already seen, it is impossible to sit in only one part of our complex identities, as if we could choose one piece of our hyphenated selves, because we are actually formed out of all of the connections that shape us. I cannot be American without also being Asian, not to mention being a child of the British empire. I cannot be Christian without also being Hindu and Buddhist.

What should be obvious by now is that finitude is key to how we are made in the image of God. We are like God, but we are finite versions of God and that is what God intended. In the words of Gordon Kaufman: "Without the particular culture which has formed each of us in a quite specific way, we cannot exist as human at all … we … acquire particular ways of being human—particular ways of seeing and understanding ourselves, particular likes and dislikes, particular possibilities of thinking and experiencing, particular conceptions of the meaning of human life and of the nature of the world in which we live."[15] This particularity is inten-

---

13   Yong, *Pneumatology*, 57.

14   Yong, *Pneumatology*, 57.

15   Kaufman, *God*, 74.

tional to our make-up. This is how God made us. It is how we are *imago dei*.

The problem is that we make universal claims that override that particularity. Those claims view finitude as part of our sinfulness or at the very least as problematic to our *imago dei*. Finitude, like difference, is not part of our sinfulness. The way we attend to it can be. The attempt to dismiss finitude by disregarding it and trying to overcome it is what makes sin possible. It breaks the actual nature of the *imago dei*. Sin is the rejection of the particular in order to embrace a false universal.

Gordon Kaufman highlights the problem with universal claims:

> Christian faith makes certain universalistic claims: about human kind, about the world, and about God. One of the major questions with which we must come to terms … is how such claims are to be understood in light of our knowledge that they, like everything else religious and cultural, have emerged within highly particular historical developments, and thus are in a significant sense relative to those developments.[16]

We need to see our particularity as part of a whole network of particular relationships, rather than as a universal that attempts to be whole on its own. Fernandez suggests that to do this, we have to pay attention to the present and how and why we are broken rather than whole.

> Shifting our hermeneutical eye to the earth or to the cosmos requires deconstruction of some of the theologies we have inherited. Instead of focusing on sin as

---

[16]   Kaufman, *God*, 75.

> primarily a rebellion against God, I agree with Majorie Hewitt Suchocki's position that sin is primarily the violation of creation, and thus a 'rebellion against creations' well-being.' Sin is a violation or the breaking of the web of life that sustains us and makes us whole, it is the violation of right relation … Yes sin is also a violation against God, but we discern this violation through our sinful constructions. It is a violation against God only if we begin to see the world, following Sallie McFague, as God's body. We sin against God because we sin against God's body. Sin is 'living a lie' in relation to the members of God's body.[17]

We cannot see those lies we are living by using our particular biohistorical wisdom to create universals in an idealized imaginary past that we then project into an idealized imaginary future. Rather, we need to look at the violations against creation that an overfocus on our particularity and fear of the mysteries of plurality create. Our failure to relate to God's body has a great deal to do with our disregard of our finitude to make a false wholeness. We do this in one of three ways: we make our particular comprehension of the *anthropos* universal and dismiss all other conceptions (as we see in the exclusivist model in the theology of religions[18] often found in the religions of the Fertile Crescent), we absorb other conceptions into our own (as we see in the inclusivist model that we tend to find in the religions that arose out of the Indus Valley), or we dismiss the biohistorical wisdom that comes from our particularity and

---

[17]   Fernandez, *Reimagining,* 55–56.

[18]   All references to different models in the theology of religions are drawn from Gavin D'Costa, *Theology and Religious Pluralism* (Oxford: Basil Blackwell, 1986).

conform ourselves to the biohistorical wisdom of another. This third possibility is what happens, for example, when a colonized person or people allow themselves to submit to the colonizing vision, whether by rejecting their own vision to take on the colonizers' or allowing their vision to be absorbed into the colonizers'. In all of these cases, the wisdom from certain particularities is lost. True wholeness of the body of God is found when all the particularities are taken seriously and contribute to the larger dynamic relationship of the whole.

Liberation, then, is living into our biohistorical particularity in a manner that does not abrogate difference but rather honors it and relates through it. Liberation from this viewpoint also means championing all the pieces of God's creation that are silenced or dismissed and resisting those who use their particularity to override others and claim dominance. To put it simply, plurality is the space where liberation is found because it is where our true humanity can thrive.

CHAPTER 5

CHURCHES AS CHAMPIONS OF DIALOGUE

What is the Church as a particular kind of community in a world that is plural and what kind of work are we asked to do in such a world? These are questions of ecclesiology and missiology. I concur with Emil Brunner when he says, "The Church exists by mission just as fire exists by burning."[1] So, who we are and what our purpose is are intricately tied together.

D. Preman Niles proposes an image of the Church in relation to the rest of the world as "the people of God in the midst of all God's people."[2] He draws this theme from

---

[1]   Emil Brunner, *The Word and the World* (London: SCM Press, 1931), 108.

[2]   This formula was proposed by Niles and used at the Theological Roundtable Sponsored by the Christian Conference of Asia (CCA) and the Council for World Mission (CWM) in Hong Kong, 1999 as a means to understand the Church's mission in the world. It was later developed by Niles in his article, "Towards the Fullness of Life: Intercontextual Relationships in Mission," *International Review of Mission* XCI, no. 363.

71

among the available biblical themes describing the relationship of the nation (*laos*) of Israel and/or Church to the nations (*ethne*), the rest of the world.[3] Our tradition tends to emphasize the theme of the *laos* (nation) *against* the *ethne* (nations), largely due to the prophetic oracles. The nation of Israel and/or the Church (seen as the people of God) is pitted against the nations, who are seen as outside of God and God's people, meaning they are damned unless they are brought into the fold.[4]

However, there are other biblical views of the relationship of the *laos* (nation) and the *ethne* (nations).[5] The Bible sometimes sees the *ethne* as against the *laos* where the *ethne* are used as a corrective punishment against the *laos*. For example, in Isaiah 10:5, the prophet claims Assyria is the tool of God's punishment of Israel. In other places in the Bible, the *laos* is called to be a blessing to the *ethne*. For example, in Genesis 12:1–3, God blesses Abram in order for him to be a blessing to those around him. The same theme is found in the book of Acts. The other side of this theme occurs as well when the *ethne* is seen as a blessing to the *laos*. This blessing can mean that the nations help preserve Israel, as in Jeremiah 29:4–15 where the text advises the exiled Israelites to see Babylon as a new home and refuge and be a blessing

---

3   D. Preman Niles, "The Word of God and the People of Asia" in *Understanding the Word: Essays in Honor of Bernhard W. Anderson*, Journal for the Study of the Old Testament, Supplement Series 37, eds. James T. Butler, Edgar W. Conrad, and Ben C. Ollenburger (Sheffield, England: JSOT Press, 1985), 307.

4   Niles, "Word," 307.

5   These alternative models of the relationship between the *laos* and the *ethne* and the examples that follow are also from D. Preman Niles, "Toward the Fullness of Life," 307–308.

to the state while there. The nations can also be a blessing by acting as liberators, as in Isaiah 44:28–45:5 where Cyrus of Persia is called by God to liberate Israel from captivity and rebuild Jerusalem. The Bible also explores the theme of the *laos* as one nation among the *ethne* (many nations) who God cares for. God sees the *ethne* on their own terms. For example, in Isaiah 19:23–25, Assyria, Egypt, and Israel are seen as working together and in Amos 9:7, God is noted not only for liberating Israel from Egypt but also for liberating the Philistines from Caphtor and the Armenians from Kir. In the New Testament, we can recognize this theme in Acts 10 where Peter, after his encounter with Cornelius, declares that God shows no partiality to any single nation. The Christian canon ends in Revelation with a vision of "the nations come into the heavenly city without prior intervention of Israel or of the Church in their histories."[6]

Niles uses his idea of the "people of God in the midst of all God's people" to invite all of these themes to be a part of the conversation of the possible relationships between the Church (*laos*) and the rest of God's creation (*ethne*), rather than just emphasizing the theme of the Church (*laos*) against the nations (*ethne*). The Church is asked to be a community that is a part of the communities they have been placed in. We are meant to be embodied in our local communities and our local communities are meant to be embodied in us, like salt in food or sugar in tea, rather than the Church being insulated and isolated from the surrounding communities. We are a people who are blessed and are meant to be a blessing by being a support and corrective to those around us and in turn allowing ourselves to

---

6   Niles, "Toward the Fullness of Life," 307–308.

be supported and corrected by them. Since the Church embodies in different contexts, the Church itself will be plural in expression.

The problem is that the Church is more interested in its institutional unity than its plural nature. The 1999 Theological Roundtable Report for the Council for World Mission and the Christian Conference of Asia notes that churches overfocus on, "the 'one' over the 'many' and 'unity' over 'harmony.'"[7] The desire in the Church is to try and find a single vision of who we are with which to absorb or dismiss all other visions.

We use Christ as a universal theological idea in order to domesticate and unify the rest of the world under our Christian banner. We even do that to our vision of the divine and, as the 1999 Report comments, we do it at the expense of other members of the Trinity.[8] Rather than seeing the value of the Creator and the Spirit and what they bring to our understanding of the Trinity on their own terms, we see them only as aids to Christ. It is as if the Trinity were a tyrannosaurs-rex, where Christ is the body of the dinosaur and its two tiny, and rather ineffectual, arms represent God and the Holy Spirit. Let us look at this in terms of the language metaphor used in chapter 3 and think of language as a means of exploring how we have constructed Christology.

---

[7]   "The People of God Among All God's Peoples: Frontiers in Christian Mission, A Report from a Theological Roundtable Sponsored by The Christian Conference of Asia and the Council for World Mission," in *The People of God Among All God's Peoples: Frontiers in Christian Mission*, ed. Philip L. Wickeri (Hong Kong and London: CCA and CWM, 2000), 12.

[8]   "People of God," 23.

We presume that the language *we* make meaning in is the language through which meaning is made. We fail to see that our native language, say English, embodies differently in different contexts. For example, British English is not the same as American English or, as George Bernard Shaw is supposed to have said, England and America are "two nations divided by a common language." To presume English functions in the same way everywhere, as anyone who travels between the two nations quickly realizes, is to leave oneself open to misunderstanding and confusion. To presume English is the *only* language through which meaning is made is to fail to see that meaning is made very differently in other languages; forcing English meaning-making upon another language will again lead to confusion and misunderstanding.

Much like presuming English as a universal language, the Church tends to lean into the idea of Christ as *pantocrator* (ruler of the cosmos) and models itself after that vision. However, it is the *kenosis* of Christ, Christ as the one who empties himself of power, that allows Christ, and the Church, to be in the world. It is through *kenosis* that Christ is able to incarnate and it is through *kenosis* that the Church can become a people of God in the midst of all God's people.[9]

Also, the other members of the Trinity open us to the breadth and mystery of God and the cosmos and the relational links made possible through the Holy Spirit, giving us wisdom concerning how to be Church.[10] We noted in chapter 1 that God is mystery because God is infinite plurality.

---

9   "People of God," 24–25.

10   "People of God," 23–24.

The Church, like the rest of creation, is a finite version of the infinite God. It would make sense, then, that the Church is plural as God is plural, just in a more finite fashion. We are in reality not *Church*, but *churches*, different communities that take the vision of the divine from God's incarnation in Christ and embody that vision in different contexts.

D. Preman Niles points out that the Church has "no earthly city or land that is specially ours except the lands in which we are located."[11] Nevertheless, throughout Christian history we have claimed the contrary. We have universalized particular embodiments of community, focused on sameness in order to create a universal institution, and chastised ourselves when we failed to create it. We have claimed lands for the Church and declared particular loci like Rome, Constantinople, England, or the United States as the "New Jerusalem," or, if you will, the "City of God" from which the Church reigns both in example and in truth. Against these claims, Niles argues that "the Christian faith does not call for a specific 'Christian' geographic location to give our faith existential validity."[12] The Church, like its founder Jesus Christ, incarnates in the contexts it finds itself in and in that process illuminates and is illuminated by those contexts. As a result, the geographic location and nature of the Church is not only multiple but irreducibly plural.[13]

Like the Spirit, the Church is scattered among the nations to be a community in the midst of the world rather

---

[11]   Niles, "Toward the Fullness of Life," 478.

[12]   Niles, "Toward the Fullness of Life," 478.

[13]   "People of God," 30.

than a city on a hill.[14] The Church is a communion of communities connected across contexts as well as a connector of contexts; the Church is a bridge that, like the Spirit, makes understanding and relationship possible between different communities. Niles writes,

> The acceptance of our geographical location as a community within communities does not deny but requires us to maintain our links across the world. As Christian communities, we find our identities both within the human communities in which we are placed and across the globe with Christian communities everywhere .... We need each other so that we may learn from each other ....[15]

This not only connects churches to churches but, because the Church is embodied in its context, churches become a means of translating among contexts and so enriching relations between them.

I am reminded of an incident with a dear friend and colleague I have known for a lifetime. He is from an old Singhala Baptist family. I am from an old Tamil Methodist/Reformed family. Sri-Lanka, the nation of our birth, taught us that to really be who we are we must see ourselves over and against each other. We learned that we could only, as Samuel Huntington describes it, love who we were by hating what we were not.[16] There was a meeting where we were asked to talk about the conflicts in our country and

---

14   Niles, "Toward the Fullness of Life," 478.

15   Niles, "Toward the Fullness of Life," 481.

16   Citing a scene from Michael Dibdin's novel, *Dead Lagoon*. Samuel P. Huntington, *The Clash of Civilizations and the Remaking of World Order* (London, New York: Touchstone Books, 1966), 20.

how to make bridges across the divisions. We found ourselves in the course of the conversation moving closer to each other and grasping hands. We realized in the process it was the common convictions among the communion of communities of Christ that allowed us to form a bond. It is this bond, even more than our shared childhood at an ecumenical seminary where our fathers taught or a lifetime of shared stories and experiences, that is the foundation of our friendship. It allowed us to understand the churches that we came from and the ethnic communities to which we belonged, as well as each other's. It overrode the thinking that we could not love who we were without hating what we were not. It is clear to me, as I believe it is to him, that without this common bond between us, in the intensity of the conflict of our native land, the hate through which we learned to define ourselves would win and destroy us both, as well as the churches and communities we belong to. This is not a cheap communion that overlooks difference, but one that makes communion through difference and in so doing becomes a blessing.

The making of connections through difference is how the Church can be a blessing and being a blessing is the function of the Church. The 1999 Report states, "The Spirit of God is at work in creation, in its plural manifestation, in all places where true healing, reconciliation, and restoration take place."[17] It is also the case that the *God of the Spirit* abides in and through the chaos that provides the Breath of Life to enable healing, reconciliation, and restoration to

---

[17]   "People of God," 23.

take place.[18] The Church's function is to participate in that activity.

How do we do that? Another way to ask that is: what is our mission? Preman Niles argues that the theological setting for what the Church is meant to be can be seen through how Israel's purpose is unfolded in Genesis 1–11. He says we have a tendency to jump too quickly to Genesis 12 and the story of Israel starting with Abraham. The clear concern of God in the opening chapters of Genesis is that God's creation be sustained.[19] The desire of God is the fullness of life found in the relationship between all things. This is the language of salvation.

Salvation is about healing and wholeness. David Ford argues that the root of the meaning of salvation is health. Health, he states, refers to a range of sources that include the physical, social, political, mental, economic, environmental, moral, and spiritual among others.[20] When any part of existence is not well, health, and therefore salvation, is jeopardized.

Preman Niles addresses the text most connected with the language of salvation, John 10:1–18.[21] He notes the idea of salvation in this passage is explained in two ways. The one most often focused on is the explanation of Jesus as the gate through which the sheep enter the pasture of abundant life. However, there is another metaphor Jesus uses first where

---

[18] For more on the Holy Spirit, chaos, and the breath of life, see chapter 3.

[19] Niles, "Toward the Fullness of Life," 476–477.

[20] David Ford, *Theology: A Very Short Introduction* (Oxford: Oxford University Press, 2013), 101.

[21] Niles, "Toward the Fullness of Life," 472–474.

he calls himself the true shepherd in contrast to the hired hand. The sheep have a relationship with the shepherd and he cares for them because they are his. The hired hand only cares for the sheep to get paid. The shepherd's primary focus in relationship to the sheep is their well-being, so in times of peril he will put himself in danger. The hireling, whose main relationship to the sheep is economic rather than personal, might not put himself in danger unless the sheep's well-being affects his pay. The shepherd cares for the sheep for their own sake, the hireling does not. The illustration of the gate, seen in this light, is meant to highlight the intensity and preciousness of the relationship between Christ and creation. If the relationship is not genuine and central, the unconditional regard for the one with which one is in relationship is in jeopardy. This text is not about the correct way to make a relationship but a description of what authentic relationship looks like. The focus on the metaphor of Jesus as the gate over Jesus as the shepherd leads us to focus on the manner by which the relationship is made instead of the relationship itself. It is rather like an Emily Post Instructional Manual on etiquette with its guidelines on proper behavior.[22] It presumes that following the proper guidelines of behavior will make for a healthy society, without delving into what the substance of healthy

---

[22] The Emily Post Instructional Manual was used in the nineteenth century in the United States to instruct immigrants on how to fit into American society. Notice the imperialistic and colonizing, not to mention, elitist nature of this practice. It is not about the practice of making a community whole by seeing the wonderful particularities and letting it contribute to the view of a healthy society in which all participate in it, but fitting all into one universal imperialistic structure.

society and societal relationship is. The first metaphor in John 10 of Jesus as the shepherd points to the substance of relationship. The second metaphor of Jesus as the gate is about the manner of making that relationship possible, and as such is secondary to the genuine substance of the relationship itself. If the manner by which the relationship is made leads to an actually healthy (life-giving) relationship, then it's well and good. However, if it does not, if the manner in which the relationship is made leads you askew, or another manner is more life-giving, it should be abandoned or substituted to get to the actual healthy relationship itself. The result of authentic, personal relationships is the promotion of the fullness of life that God intends. This is consistent with Jesus's stated purpose that he came that we might, "have life and have it abundantly" (John 10:10). If salvation is about healing and wholeness, then, as the 1999 Report points out, any understanding of salvation as separating the world into the reached and the damned is inconsistent with the original sense of the term.[23]

The work of the churches, our mission, then flows from the work of God. What we need is, "a missiology that affirms the many ways in which God relates to peoples, and the many ways in which humankind has responded to God."[24] To do this work, we have to understand what our particular contribution is to the larger conversation of how God relates to and blesses the cosmos. We need to understand the implications of incarnation. Namely, Jesus Christ is the particular means that allows Christians to understand God. Jesus Christ, to use a previous metaphor, is our language of

---

[23]   "People of God," 17.

[24]   "People of God," 12.

understanding and meaning-making. In other words, Jesus is, as Lakshman Wickremesinghe says, central and normative to how we as Christians understand the world, but the wisdom of Jesus Christ is not complete and total.[25] As the 1999 Report states, for the Church, Jesus Christ shows how God loves the world and how we connect to this world through the Holy Spirit.[26] The report goes on to say that God did not just become a human being, but a poor Jew and that this has implications for the mission of the churches.[27] Therefore, being a blessing as God was as seen in Jesus Christ, means being a blessing for the oppressed.[28] We do this by making space for those with the least power. The impulse to make a central and normative vision complete and total is done at the expense of the ones that do not have the power to assert their central and normative visions. As has been stated before, to assert one's vision over others, one needs the power to do so.

The Church, for the very reason that it sees Jesus Christ as the central and normative way to understand God's relationship to the world and that Jesus Christ stands with the ones without power, must seek solidarity with the powerless as well. In other words, being Church means we must make space for plurality because that is the means to allow for the weakest voices to be heard.

---

[25] See Lakshman Wickremesinghe, "Togetherness and Uniqueness-Living Faiths in Inter-Relation," *CTC Bulletin*, vol. 5, no. 1–2 (April-August, 1984), 7.

[26] "People of God," 12-13.

[27] "People of God," 24–25.

[28] "People of God," 41.

Niles calls this mission in contestation.[29] By this, he means that churches need to read the signs of the times and champion the voices that allow for the largest amount of plurality and contest the ones who deny it. This, he feels, is what is behind the idea in John 10:10 of having life abundantly. Ironically, it has become the text that is used to negate plurality and privilege a single vision. He writes,

> Our salvation, *shalom*, well being, is mixed up with the salvation of the nations. We have a dual identity: the identity of our faith and the identity of the people in the midst of whom we live. To relate these two identities is an inevitable part of understanding mission as contestation toward the fullness of life.[30]

Contestation then is seen in relationship to the powers that deny life. It is the resistance to the myth of pure identity and the corresponding assumption, named by Samuel Huntington, that unless I hate what I am not I cannot love what I am. The 1999 Report states that mission in contestation calls out all religions, especially our own, which have functioned in ways that deny the dignity and freedom of peoples. It demands that we be held accountable to all that have been excluded and marginalized by the expression of who we are and the work we do.[31]

The function of the Church is to remove the powers and structures that deny abundant life to the people and remove the barriers and hindrances that prevent the offer

---

29   Niles, "Toward the Fullness of Life," 474–475.

30   Niles, "Toward the Fullness of Life," 478.

31   "People of God," 27.

of abundant life from reaching people.[32] In other words, the work of the Church is a liberative activity.

The way this activity takes place is by being in the midst of the people we want to relate to. The Church does not have a privileged position, but it does have a particular vision that can allow us to see the other visions around us and recognize their value. To assume privilege mutes, if not eradicates, that particularity by taking that particular vision and making it universal. We have often assumed that if we do not assert Christ as a universal vision for all, then Christ has no real meaning for the world. In asserting Christ as universal, however, we abandon the example of Jesus, who moved among the margins of society, and the meaning of the incarnation, where God abandons all claims of divine privilege to become human. The irony is that by moving our vision of Jesus to the center of power, the very unique insights we have in Jesus are lost.

Niles believes the paradigm of "being in the midst," of being a particular one among many, allows us to take a stance of openness and receptiveness that is needed to overcome suspicion.[33] It also helps us to lead nations to learn from one another and in so doing, come to a deeper understanding and appreciation of God's purpose for the whole creation. It is only with an honest humility that we can understand who we are and through which we can appreciate our own particular vision of God. It is from this particular vision that we are able to have the generosity to interact with the other ways to see the wonders of God and God's creation.

---

[32] Niles, "Toward the Fullness of Life," 474.

[33] Niles, "Toward the Fullness of Life," 480.

A CONCLUDING INVITATION

It is my assumption in this book that Christianity has largely understood itself in conversation with empire. In its early period, Christianity understood itself as resistant and counter to empire. Later, it became a companion and an apologetic of empire and throughout history, it has seen itself as the true empire. As a result of its engagement with empire, it has seen other faiths as competition.

Christian faith, as a result, has been set up to be the only option, the best option, or the only meaningfully relevant option. No matter what, it is always the superior option, making the conversation with other faiths, at worst, antagonistic and dismissive or, at best, patronizing and controlling.

This book offers ruminations on Christian doctrine so that it can be a conversation partner with other faiths. It tries to think about Christian doctrine in a manner that sees openness to other faiths as inherent to Christian faith being true to itself. This means that Christian doctrine also takes itself seriously and figures out what values it has to share in the conversation. Finally, it assumes, by doing so, that Christian doctrine actually becomes liberative.

What this book is not is an apologetic for Christianity and how it has been done in the past, nor a correct set of alternative ways of doing theology. It is rather a contemplation and an invitation to think of the Christian faith in ways that take the pluralism around us seriously. It looks at the scholarship of those who have seen and been open to such plurality and uses it to propose a different way of constructing Christian doctrine.

All of this is merely a beginning and needs other scholars from the tradition, preferably in conversation with other traditions, to press it further, nuance it, and see what consequences it has for how we think about and practice our faith.

INDEX

Thangaraj, Thomas 44
theology of religions 40, 68
  Exclusivist model 27
  Inclusivist model 28
Thomas, M. M. 40
Tower of Babel 9, 53
Tracy, David v, 26, 27, 43, 55
Trinidad, Saúl 23
Trinity 15, 45, 74, 75

V

Victor Premsagar 63
Vivekananda 29, 30
Von Rad, Gerhard 52

W

Wickremesinghe, Lakshman
      5, 12, 14, 47, 82

Y

Yong, Amos 44, 46, 50, 65